Complying with Genocide

Complying with Genocide

The Wolf You Feed

E. N. Anderson and Barbara A. Anderson

LEXINGTON BOOKS

Lanham • Boulder • New York • London

Published by Lexington Books
An imprint of The Rowman & Littlefield Publishing Group, Inc.
4501 Forbes Boulevard, Suite 200, Lanham, Maryland 20706
www.rowman.com

6 Tinworth Street, London SE11 5AL, United Kingdom

British Library Cataloguing in Publication Information Available

Library of Congress Cataloging-in-Publication Data Available

Library of Congress Control Number: 2020942608

ISBN 978-1-7936-3459-7 (cloth)
ISBN 978-1-7936-3461-0 (pbk)
ISBN 978-1-7936-3460-3 (electronic)

In gratitude to the good wolves in our life,
our many beloved dogs who have taught us
tolerance as we inadvertently stepped on their paws,
trust when we were fearful, and
love in a world filled with hatred.

Contents

Preface

"My child, it's time to teach you the most important lesson about life and people. It is that everyone has within two wolves: a good wolf that wants to help everyone and do what's best for all, and a bad wolf that wants to do evil and hurt people and the world."

"Father, that's scary. It really worries me. Which wolf wins out in the end?" asked the child.

The father replied, "The wolf you feed."

Native American folktale

This story—perhaps more Manichaean than Native American—captures much of what we have learned in our lives. We were both raised to think of people as both good and evil. People around us failed to substantiate that premise. In fact, people were often quite deliberately bad. Many ordinary people hurt themselves just to hurt real or imagined foes. They ruined relationships because of imagined or trivial slights. They voted their own destruction by electing people who promised to crush "the others." They sacrificed their lives for extremist causes.

While some persons rise to being saintly, most people are neutral, neither saintly nor demonic, but rather vacillating between working with or against others. They may be virtuous: helping, sheltering, caring and vicious: excluding, ignoring, hurting. Most people are good some of the time. Even mass murderers and psychopaths may demonstrate decent behavior on occasion.

Pascal Boyer stated, "Observers from outside our species would certainly be struck by two facts about humans. They are extraordinarily good at forming groups, and they are just as good at fighting other groups" (2018:33). Constantly forced to choose which side to join, they often choose the dark side—riots, wars, genocides, mobs, raids, collective violence, murder, torture, rape, destruction. They may also collude with the dark side, albeit less directly, through dispossessing communities, exposing others to disasters or pollution, running slave markets, refusing aid to the starving, or selling cigarettes in mass campaigns. Yet, these less visible perpetrators still choose cold-blooded, systematic killing. Leaders point the way as many follow— killing friends, neighbors, and fellow citizens without compunction and often with no conceivable personal benefit. Despite claims of moral progress, the genocidal dictator and the suicide bomber are powerful emblems of the late twentieth and early twenty-first century.

Most killers were good citizens before succumbing to the bad wolf. Then, back in ordinary life, they feed the good wolf, again becoming peaceable, neighborly people. Most children do not inherently hate, but must be taught, very carefully taught, to hate (B. Anderson in D. Baker [ed.] *Make us One*, 1995). Unlike Thomas Hobbes (1950 [1651]) who proposed that violent "warre" is the natural human state, most people, including soldiers, rarely encounter, seek or continue with violence. It takes sustained effort to create the bad wolf of genocide and killing.

Modern psychology, as well as the experience of dozens of genocides and civil wars in the last century, sheds much light on why humans have two wolves and what feeds those wolves. The nature and promotion of human good and solidarity have been addressed by every religion, and by many scientists, including psychologists. Evil is less well studied. Outside of religious imprecations against sin, there are few studies, mostly by psychologists. Key studies are noted.

We are struck by the chilling familiarity of the few portraits of humans as changing from one state to the other. We have drawn heavily on Shakespeare, ever the greatest chronicler of human frailty, in our work, and especially on *Othello*, surely the world's greatest and most shattering record of a man's descent into hell at the instigation of an evil manipulator. *Othello* contains every theme and conclusion of our book, from racism to greed, revenge, and personal loss. Robert Louis Stevenson's "Dr. Jekyll and Mr. Hyde" is classic. In Hermann Hesse's harrowing novel, *Steppenwolf*, the mild-mannered Harry Haller confronts the savage steppe wolf inside himself in the chaos of post-World War I Germany (Hesse 2002 [1927]). Likewise, there are disturbing memoirs of ordinary people caught up in genocides, as in China, Rwanda, and Cambodia. Most persons claim to have no idea how they could suddenly violate every moral rule and shred of decency. The frequently maligned wolf emerges as a common metaphor.

Domesticated wolves become dogs: social, generally peaceable and friendly creatures. Their killer instincts, however, may suddenly surface in hunting, in defense, in fights for pack dominance, and sometimes for what seem to be trivial reasons, as dog and wolf trainers know well. Their hunting behavior is cool, rational, careful; their defensive behavior vicious. What dogs and wolves do *not* do, however, is form vast movements of unrelated strangers within their species simply to kill, loot, and destroy others of their species.

This is our third work on the enigmatic nature of genocide. Our first work, *Warning Signs of Genocide: An Anthropological Perspective* (2012), was a comprehensive review of the history of genocide and the development of an explanatory, predictive model based upon this historical record. In our second book, *Halting Genocide in America: An Anthropological Perspective* (2017), we examined the risk for genocide under the current policy directions and political landscape in the United States. In this third volume, we investigate the phenomenon of conforming to genocide building upon the metaphor of feeding the wolf.

Targeted toward scholars and persons concerned with human evil, this work examines human evil and complicity in mass killing, analyzes genocide trends over time, and discusses ethical frameworks and strategies to counter conformity to genocide.

Eugene and Barbara Anderson
Riverside, California, 2020

Acknowledgments

We would like to thank many colleagues who provided valuable comments, in particular Christopher Chase-Dunn, Peter Grimes, Hollie Nyseth Brehm, Jennifer Dudley, Andrea Wilson, and Rebecca Alvarez. We express our gratitude to our parents, siblings, friends, and mentors for modeling social justice and supporting our interest in this difficult topic. Lastly, to our children, you give us reason to fight for a future where the good wolf is fed.

Part I

MASS KILLING

THE STORY OF COMPLICITY

"Is this a dagger which I see before me, the handle toward my hand?"

William Shakespeare
(Macbeth Act 2, Scene 1)

Chapter 1

Genocide

GENOCIDE DEFINED

Visiting Cambodia together in the late 1990s, we saw the relics of genocide and the devastation it had wrought. Barbara (BA) had done her doctoral work with Cambodian refugee women and worked in the border camps in Thailand, but she did not step across the Cambodian border until later when she worked with the World Health Organization. Our visit was a journey to remember and to affirm our commitment to study genocide together.

At that time, little was known about genocide in general. Thousands of historical sources covered Hitler's Holocaust, and a much smaller but still important literature covered the mass killings by the Young Turks, the USSR leadership, and Mao Zedong. Much more recent genocides, such as those in ex-Yugoslavia, Rwanda, and Cambodia itself, were beginning to be visible in scholarly sources.

Very few generalizations had come out of the scholarly work on genocide. Rudolph Rummel wrote *Death by Government* (1994) and *Statistics of Democide* (1998), arguing that genocide was the natural result of totalitarian regimes. His oft-repeated conclusion was direct: "Power kills; absolute Power kills absolutely" (Rummel 1994:1).

We quickly realized that he was not far wrong, but that was not quite the whole story. Hitler was democratically elected, although he committed genocide only after taking total power. Several other notorious genociders have been democratically elected. They usually seized absolute power and then began killing, but often did not seize total power until the killing was under way. Some genuine democracies have committed genocide. We embarked on a voyage of discovery, comparing all documented genocides since 1900 and searching for common themes.

When science reaches this stage—several teams working on a problem—
one expects simultaneous discoveries, and this is what occurred. Barbara
Harff (2012), ourselves (Anderson and Anderson 2013, 2017), and shortly
after us, Hollie Nyseth Brehm (2017a), independently developed the same
basic model of genocide. James Waller, in his great work *Confronting Evil*
(2016), has developed it further. Gregory Stanton's well-known list of traits
of genocide (2013) is another independent invention of a similar model. (See
these sources, especially Anderson and Anderson 2013; Waller 2016, for
reviews of the literature on genocide.)

Genocide is quite consistent. A would-be leader wins by marshaling ethnic
and ideological hate, but goes beyond hate to promise a utopian world. The
leader harks back to a lost golden age and promises to restore and improve
it—*if only* "certain people" could be eliminated. The largest and most indiscriminate genocides were carried out by fascists (Hitler being the extreme
case), communists (Stalin, Mao, and others), or more rarely, ethnic fanatics
(Rwanda) or religious zealots (Iran). Military dictators and juntas routinely
kill opponents, but without at least some background in fascism, they tend
to be oppressive but not genocidal. Hitler-sympathizing militaries lay behind
the genocidal regimes of Suharto in Indonesia (the army was trained by
pro-Hitler Dutch), Rios Montt in Guatemala, and others. The colonels in
Argentina in the 1970s made *Mein Kampf* required reading for officers'
training (Timmerman 2002). Less ideological military regimes are usually
repressive but not so extreme, for example, Egypt where the genocide of the
Copts has been prevented. There are truly genocidal military tyrants without
notable ideological identification, as in modern Burma and in Saddam's Iraq.

Barbara Harff, whose model appeared first and therefore is the most often
quoted, refers to "exclusionary ideologies," ideologies that privilege some
over others (2012). These ideologies may be religious (Wahhabism, right-
wing Christianity), political (communism, fascism), ethnic or "racial" (anti-
Semitism), class (anti-poor persons), sexual orientation (anti-LGBTQ), or
other. The common theme is that one group of people is highly valued while
another is devalued or actively hated. The level of devaluing may be simple
ignoring, as when local people obstructing "progress" are cleared out with
bulldozers (Scudder 2005). More visible and universal in major genocides is
the hysterical hatred typified by Hitler's speeches. The common theme is that
some people do not deserve to exist.

Such ideologies, and their leading exponents, often flourish when difficult
and uncertain times give people economic incentives to look for radical solutions. Particularly risky are wars, including civil wars and wars of liberation,
because an amoral, power-hungry despot can easily develop an appetite for
blood and ascend to power through conflict. However, many evil leaders
take power in good times; mobilizing antagonism is always available as

an easy, straightforward way to win in politics. All that is required is that the existing administration is widely perceived as corrupt and incompetent. People then work for change. Commonly, the country in question had a long record of ethnic and political killing, but this was not always the case. Although genocidal regimes have arisen under many circumstances, we can predict that a strong and successful regime in a functioning democracy is relatively safe.

This simple model—exclusionary ideology, dictatorship, consolidation, and challenge—turns out to be highly predictive (Anderson and Anderson 2013; Nyseth Brehm 2017a). It models genocide under the strictest construction of Raphael Lemkin's definition of the term (see Waller 2016)—the actual mass murder of innocent citizens or subjects by their own government, or cultural extermination by forced acculturation and other restrictions. Genocide, by its very nature, is hard to define or separate from other kinds of war, and arguments about definition go on endlessly. Lemkin's definition can be seen as "hegemonic," as argued by Benjamin Meiches (2019). We restrict ourselves to the narrow definition here. In the narrow Lemkin definition, genocide is usually rather simple: when autocratic leaders feel they are in a shaky situation, they kill. Very often—famously with Hitler, Stalin, and Mao—they come to depend more and more on the level of hatred of their supporters, and thus must whip up more hate to stay in power, to provide red meat to their "base." This is a tactic well known to demagogic politicians, and only the lack of total autocratic power of the ruler saves minorities in many a nation today.

This model has been extended and nuanced by one of its creators, Hollie Nyseth Brehm (2020). She points out, in a masterful review of the prediction literature, that contemporary genocide is not always done by the state; it can be done by internationally operated terrorist groups, for example, ISIL in the Middle East, and militias (such as the many that operate in eastern Democratic Republic of the Congo). In her research on Rwanda, she shows that one must compare the actual conflict situations and regional differences, which can be striking within a country whose central government is totally committed to genocide everywhere.

By contrast, some of the best studies of genocide are far broader. They include all mass killing of civilians in war. Since every war known in history involves some massacre of civilians, this makes genocide simply a part of most wars. Ben Kiernan (2007) and Martin Shaw (2013) used this wider definition in their excellent histories of mass killing. Our model does not work for this extended use of the term. One would have to have a predictive model of all war—something that has so far defied scholarship. Wars are notoriously multicausal; it usually takes several reasons to make leaders decide to go to war. Economic gain (or acquisition of resources and land), increasing political power of the state or its leaders, ethnic and religious conflicts, traditions of warrior culture, and other factors can all be decisive.

Genocide and war always include far more than mere killing. Victims are routinely tortured. Women and girls are raped. People are burned or buried alive. The deliberate sadism goes beyond anything an ordinary creative torturer could devise. There have been instruction books on torturing for centuries, and there are now websites on the "dark web." Ordinary people are as prone to do all this as the leaders themselves. Similar findings are common in studies of warfare, criminal gangs (Baumeister 1997), and perhaps above all the whole history of heresy persecution in religions.

Ordinary people caught up in even the most mundane street gangs soon learn to commit unspeakable acts without second thoughts. Psychological explanations of this range from direct explanations in terms of conformity, anger, learned hate, and social antipathy (Baron-Cohen 2011; Baumeister 1997) to the elaborate (and improbable) Freudian–Lacanian framework of Edward Weisband (2017, 2019). Mobs, genocides, and wars do not just happen, and they are not the result of blind forces. They are invoked by individuals. People do not spontaneously go into orgies of murder, unless some leaders are profiting in important ways. Whipping up hatred is not confined to leaders—anyone can do it—but ordinary people doing it at grassroots levels can do only so much damage. With leadership, they can form large, far-reaching organizations like Hitler's Nazis, the Ku Klux Klan, or the Khmer Rouge.

Further work since 2012 has extended genocide models backward, defining factors that led to extreme abuse of autocratic power and resultant genocide. Waller's *Confronting Evil* (2016) and Dikötter's *How to Be a Dictator* (2019) posit that the widely targeted genocides of modern times accompany the decline of traditional societies, the rise of mass communication, and the installment of top-down social structures. Links evolve from networks of local people to government authority that assumes escalating power, even in democratic societies.

Plantation slavery or serfdom is a back story. Developed in ancient Mesopotamia, it was the first institution based on cruel treatment of disenfranchised multitudes by ruling elites. It grew steadily, especially in the West, peaking in the trans-Atlantic slave trade and the indentured-labor plantations of Asia in the eighteenth and nineteenth centuries. It led to a vast amount of murder. Slavery, though not in itself genocide by the narrow definition, is very close to it, and requires a similar mentality: the basic idea that one whole group of humans does not deserve human consideration. By establishing that mindset, it helped the progress to modern genocide. The slave trade was notoriously bloody. Even though the purpose of slavery was coerced labor, sometimes it crossed into outright genocide.

Today, genocide continues around the globe, as in Myanmar, Sudan, and South Sudan. Turkey, Syria, and Iraq have joined in attempting genocide of the Kurds (covered in detail in *Genocide Studies International* 13:1, 2019; see Joeden-Forgey and McGee 2019). China is committing genocide against its Uyghur population. It has imprisoned a million and killed an unknown number (Byler 2018; Stavrou 2019). China is also repressing Tibetans, Mongols, Kazakhs, and Hui, apparently to crush religious and cultural minorities even though China's surveillance system has seemed to establish that these minorities are not a security risk. Turkish repression of Kurds, Indonesian treatment of Papuans, and Brazilian massacres of Indigenous people are reaching genocidal proportions. Violent or potentially genocidal regimes now control about one-sixth of the world's nations. Genocide is highly contingent on context. According to the predictors above, over a dozen countries are on the brink, but currently only a few are actively genocidal.

DICTATORS AND GENOCIDE

Many dictators have ridden popular movements to victory, but many were installed by large economic interests, almost always rentiers—landlords, natural resource owners, and others who make their money from controlling primary production rather than from enterprise. Oil has been the greatest single backer of modern autocratic states (Auzanneau 2018), from fascist (several in Africa and elsewhere) to feudal (Saudi Arabia) to socialist (Venezuela). Some genocides have direct corporate backing. American corporations influenced the CIA in establishing genocidal regimes in Guatemala, El Salvador, and Chile (see, for example, Saucier and Akers 2018). European colonial powers sometimes established murderous, genocidal successor regimes in liberated colonies, or, conversely, set up weak local governments that soon fell to genocidal rebels. Former colony status is a fair predictor of genocide. In the mid-twentieth century, most dictators were puppets installed by fascist or communist regimes. In addition, the United States installed or backed several genocidal fascist regimes, most notably in Guatemala and Chile (see the history of twentieth-century genocides in Anderson and Anderson 2013; Kiernan 2007; Rummel 1994, 1998; Shaw 2013).

Many genocidal regimes have survived and flourished despite mass murder because states support business interests that are benefited by the regimes in question. Cases range from early fascist Italy under Mussolini to more modern states such as Nigeria and Equatorial Guinea. The oil industry is notorious for this (Auzanneau 2018), as is armaments trading. Related are the violence-sourced "blood diamonds" in Angola and elsewhere, and blood coltan (columbium–tantalum ore) in the Democratic Republic of the Congo.

However, there is no definite link between dictatorship, genocide, and any particular economic system, organization, interest, or condition. Feudal, capitalist, socialist, "neoliberal," militarist, theocratic, and communist countries have all done it. Ancient and medieval empires and modern states of all political and ideological frameworks did it. Claims that genocide is most likely during economic downturns or is associated with deprivation do not hold up (Anderson and Anderson 2013; Nyseth Brehm 2017a, 2017b). This point is critical to all that follows. Economic explanations do not account for even a part of the variance in genocide incidence, at least from these comprehensive models developed from different databases. Economic motivations often drive some supporters, including powerful ones, and ties to primary production and heavy industry are often clear, but these are usually post hoc. They are developed by the leaders and their exclusionary movements *after* the movements have gained traction. Hatred, not economics, explains autocratic regimes and genocide.

Before 1945, mass bloodshed was generally dominated by world wars. Since then, most genocidal and autocratic regimes have come to power through coups, local wars, or often elections, causing more deaths than all wars, murders, and crimes combined. Democracy has even been considered a risk factor (Mann 2005), but this is highly dubious; mass killing always awaits seizing of autocratic power (Rummel 1994, 1998). Corrupt and weak regimes create conditions where many will vote for strongmen. Hitler had real strongman power, his American imitators very little before 2017.

The notorious dictators—the ones who launched vast, multitargeted genocides—were self-made, fighting their way up via extremist organizations. Hitler, Stalin, Mao, and several lesser, but still mass-murderous figures chronicled by Frank Dikötter in *How to Be a Dictator* (2019) shared ruthless monomania in pursuit of power, targeted hatred, and a cult of personality that escalated out of control. Such excesses and irrational decisions, as in Hitler's case, eventually prove fatal. Irrational actions begin as bravado, the *locura* of street Spanish: acting crazy and destructive to terrorize or daunt others. Such people may be more than a little mad, but usually they are carefully calculating the level of their risk-taking and aggressiveness. The problem is that acting slowly drifts over into believing. Dictators who pretend to be divine and infallible, and act irrationally to demonstrate it, often come to believe their own stories, acting genuinely irrational to the point of self-destruction.

On the other hand, harsh military men who take autocratic control and begin systematic murder are usually of a more realistic, grim, coldly "rational" sort. Examples are Chile's Pinochet, Spain's Franco, and the military dictators of Egypt. They generally engage in targeted but not mass extermination. Very common are genociders somewhere in the middle, coldly rational yet driven by extremism and delusion. This seems to have been the case with the Argentine colonels of the mid-1970s (Timmerman 2002).

Ron Rosenbaum, in *Explaining Hitler* (2014), argues against facile ad hoc explanations and defining Hitler (and by extension other genociders) as uniquely and to some extent incomprehensibly evil, an extremist, self-deluding narcissist leader. Ordinary bullies generally know their actions are bad and negatively judged, creating guilt and/or resentment or they are psychopathic enough to feel no guilt and to resent the judgments of others. Either way, they may go out of their way to be harmful and hateful, as we have witnessed among right-wing extremists and in the extreme political and religious movements everywhere. Genociders are skilled bullies.

John Kincaid says of American far-right politics, "right-wing movements are successful when they deploy rhetorical frames that synthesize both material and symbolic politics" (Kincaid 2016:529), and this finding summarizes a fact that seems well documented worldwide. Oliver Hahl and collaborators (2018) have shown that "lying demagogues" succeed when disaffected voters feel disrespected by elites and intellectuals. Dictators often combine lying, violating norms, openly expressing taboo but widely held prejudices, and economic populism. Donald Trump is one of many leaders who triumphed in the early twenty-first century by using this technique.

When a dictator takes over, he (such leaders are usually male, so far) quickly moves to consolidate power. He can usually bring about a brief return of prosperity by cracking down on crime and by "making the trains run on time" (as in the popular claim for Mussolini), but that prosperity may be illusory or short-lived. Alternatively, the leader may take over during a war, in which case he may lead the people to victory, or may simply make things even worse, as in Cambodia. He suspends whatever democratic or institutional checks exist. Many smaller scale genocides have taken place in democracies, but often the victims were not citizens and were under de facto authoritarian rule instead of participating in the democracy. Native Americans in the nineteenth century constitute a prime example. A contemporary example is the humanitarian crisis among migrants on the southern border of the United States.

A dictator almost inevitably begins to consolidate his rule by killing "certain people"—whether they are Jews, bourgeoisie, political enemies, educated people, "heretics," or any other salient group that seems opposed in some way to the new order. We term these persons "structural opponent groups." They are usually traditionally disliked minorities, but they may be local political enemies, new rivals, or ideological or ethnic opposites. When a dictator seizes control, he can quickly draw on his power, on the loyalty of his base, and on lack of countervailing horizontal forces. He can rapidly turn a peaceful, orderly society into a killing machine.

However, he can only do so if he has both public and financial support. Many genocides are enabled by specific firms or economic interests, usually primary-production interests, or heavy manufacturers as in Nazi Germany. Some communist genocides have taken place with support from peasants and workers rather than giant firms, but others had support from giant state-owned economic interests.

Dictators who invoke genocides are a special selection (Dikötter 2019). Many genocidal leaders fall into two types. Most are elites, but a surprisingly number of them are marginal—subalterns or regional derived, educated in contexts that are also somewhat marginal (often from military academies), members of small popular fascists movements, or mentored by extremists, radicals, or lovers of violence (see Anderson and Anderson 2013; Rosenbaum 2014; Waller 2016).

Exemplars include Napoleon (Corsican), Stalin (Georgian), Hitler (remote-rural Austrian), Mao (educated in Japan), and the Cambodian genocide leaders (educated in Paris with mentoring by the Egyptian Samir Amin). Some were short or disfigured, or similarly socially challenged (see Dikötter 2019 for several cases). This compensation theory of problematic behavior and socially challenged appearance has a long history and literature. It is not a total explanation, but it has been abundantly noted, qualified, and nuanced (Baumeister 1997). Many of the genociders have been military men: Napoleon the corporal, the Argentine colonels, General Rios Montt in Guatemala, and Idi Amin in Uganda come to mind. Leading in mass killing is, of course, the job of military officers.

Usually, the ideologues of these exclusionary ideologies are not themselves killers. Karl Marx dreamed revolution, but actually spent his time studying and writing in the magnificent reading room of the British Museum. Friedrich Nietzsche in Germany and Gabriele d'Annunzio in Italy were the major thinkers behind fascism, but they led scholarly lives. It was left to street toughs and low-ranking military men to become the hard-nosed opportunists that led the movements and were also the initial followers and fighters (Mann 2004; Snyder 2015). They were often animated more by hatred and ambition than by attention to doctrine.

These dictators share one quite specific ideology: the purity and superiority of one group over the abysmal badness of another, with the further concept that all members of each group have those respective essences. Genocide scholars Gerard Saucier and Laura Akers extrapolated twenty specific ideas from an extensive analysis of the rhetoric of genocide leaders in twenty of the major historic cases. They include "tactics/excuses for violence, dispositionalism/essentialism, purity/cleansing language, dehumanization, dualistic/dichotomous thinking, internal enemies, crush-smash-exterminate-eliminate [language], group or national unity, racialism in some form, xenophobia/

foreign influence, uncivilized or uncivilizable, attachment/entitlement to land, body or disease metaphor, revenge or retaliation language, traitor talk (treason, treachery, etc.), conspiracy, subversion, something held sacred, nationalism/ethnonationalism, threat of annihilation of our people" (Saucier and Akers 2018:88).

They add some other frequent themes, including "placing national security above other goals," wanting to move fast and thoroughly, and thinking "individuals must suffer for the good of the collective" (Saucier and Akers 2018:90). They find all of these examples from the rhetoric of Hitler and Stalin to the less widely known writings of the Serbian and World War II-Japanese leadership and the propaganda of mass murderers of Indigenous people in Australia and the United States. Dehumanizing terms like "rats," "cockroaches," and "insects" appear to be universal: witness the terminology used in the Rwandan genocide (Kidder 2009). The Communist Chinese leadership described Falun Gong members and other dissidents as "rats" and "subversives" (Cheung et al. 2018).

The extent of killing sometimes depends on the number of targeted groups, which in turn depends on the extremism of the dictator. Hitler's indiscriminate hatred extended from Jews, disabled people, gays, Roma, Slavs, socialists, and even modern artists. The Khmer Rouge genocide in Cambodia included anyone defined by nonmajority ethnicity, education, and foreign influence. The Rwandan genocide began with Tutsi, but quickly moved on to eliminate many Hutu (Nyseth Brehm 2017b). At the other extreme are mass political killings that eliminate the opposition and anyone related to it, but at least stop there. Such "politicides" are typical when the leader is not ideologically extreme. Agustin Pinochet's in Chile, which killed about 10,000 people, is an example. Another is Ferdinand Marcos' regime in the Philippines. These political genocides blend into the mass political elimination typical of ancient and medieval empires, in which opponents, possible opponents, and their extended families were routinely eliminated.

Once the dictator assumes power, there is often a lull in the killing. The leader has his power. Eventually, however, unrest challenges his position. In some cases, he is forced out. Dictators often fall. If they come to believe in their own personality cult, they may think they are infallible—a dangerous illusion (Dikötter 2019). Often, however, a leader meets the new challenge by another wave of mass murder. The challenge is often external war, as in Hitler's Germany and the Khmer Rouge's Cambodia. Sometimes it is power-jockeying within the ruling party, as in the USSR and Mao's China. Sometimes it is civil war or revolt, as in the Indian subcontinent when successive episodes of violence accompanied the breakaway of Pakistan from India, the later breakaway of Bangladesh from Pakistan, and the failed revolution of the Tamils in Sri Lanka.

TYPES OF GENOCIDE: HATE IN
ORGANIZED MANIFESTATIONS

There are three ways to hate: hate upward (hating the elites), down (hating the less fortunate: the poor, the less abled, the visible minorities), or laterally (real enemies or social rivals). Divisive leaders encourage their followers to hate downward—to hate the weak, the powerless, the minorities. Even those who took power by marshaling upward hate, such as the communists, have found that it pays to get their followers to hate downward. Stalin quickly moved from executing the rich to eliminating small and local ethnic groups.

Settler Genocide

Genocides fall into four types: settler, "cold," consolidation, and crisis geno-cides (our classification; see Waller 2016 for more detailed but similar typol-ogy). Settler genocides occur when a large, powerful society takes over land from small or scattered groups, especially when the powerful society is tech-nologically advanced and the smaller victim groups are less so ("Whatever happens, we have got/the Gatling gun and they have not"—Hilaire Belloc; also quoted as "Maxim gun"). This type of genocide is generally a bottom-up phenomenon as are small-scale religious massacres such as the French Terror. These genocides have occurred in the United States (Dee Brown 1971; Madley 2016), Brazil (Hemming 1978), and Australia (Pascoe 2014), as well as Russia, China, Japan, and elsewhere (Kiernan 2007 provides an excellent, comprehensive history).

This pattern reaches back in time. Ancient Babylon and Assyria extermi-nated captives. The Romans and medieval Europeans exterminated rebellious subject peoples and took their possessions. The Bantu took southern Africa from the Khoi-San with attendant exterminations. Settler genocides depended on convincing a large part of the citizenry to kill the Indigenous peoples, and to threaten protectors and dissidents into silence. A particularly good study of this is Benjamin Madley's study of California in the nineteenth century (2016).

This counts as genocide only if the victims were conquered and subjected. Extermination of enemies who are fighting back with everything they have is a global pattern of war, not genocide. The dividing line can be blurred, but extremes are easy to see. The wars with the Apaches and Comanche (Hämäläinen 2008) in the United States and Mexico in the 1870s were ini-tially straightforward wars with little quarter given by either side, and thus not genocide, but the extermination of the Yuki in California in the mid-nineteenth century was genocidal massacre of helpless conquered people (Madley 2016; Miller 1979).

"Cold" Genocide

A marginal form of settler genocide has been called "cold genocide." This is the slow elimination of an ethnic group by selective killing over a long time, coupled with every effort to destroy the group as a distinguishable entity by eliminating its culture or ideology. The term "cold genocide" was coined by Kjell Anderson (2015) to describe the Indonesian pressure on West Irian (West Papua). It has been applied to the far larger and bloodier repression of the Falun Gong movement in China since the late 1990s. This movement, a spiritual discipline that by all accounts except the Chinese governments was utterly inoffensive, seemed dangerous to the Communist leadership, because of its size and rapid growth. Suppression included propaganda wars, but also mass torture, imprisonment ("reeducation" in "camps"), and killing by extracting body parts for transplantation or the international black market (Cheung et al. 2018, citing a huge literature). Executed Falun Gong members have become the major source of hearts, livers, and other vital organs in China.

The Chinese government has now expanded its reach to include the Muslim Uighurs of Xinjiang. Approximately a million have been placed in concentration camps ("vocational training centers") and subjected to intense pressure to acculturate to Han majority norms (Byler 2018). Children have been removed from homes and parents, and educated according to Han patterns. Islam is attacked in particular. The Chinese government has accused them of ISIS-style terrorism because of a very few extreme individuals, but their real sin appears to have been agitating for minority rights guaranteed by the Chinese constitution. Recently, government agencies in Uighur territory have been ordering thousands of clubs, stock probes, tear gas canisters, spiked clubs, handcuffs, prison uniforms, and other instruments of suppression and torture (SBS News 2018).

This constitutes "culturocide," the form of genocide that involves destruction of an entire culture by restriction of personal freedoms and forced removal and reeducation of children—one of the forms of genocide specifically addressed by Lemkin. A closely related practice is "linguicide," attempted extermination of a language, usually with murder of many or most speakers; linguicide is currently being waged against the Kurds (Salih 2019) and has routinely been practiced against colonialized minorities, especially in the Americas.

Consolidation Genocide

Consolidation genocide is often among the worst. It occurs when a rather shaky totalitarian regime based on exclusionary ideology takes full control of a country. The number of deaths range widely from rather small-scale politicides (like Marcos' in the Philippines and Pinochet's in Chile) to vast mass murders (like Mao's in China). The scale depends on the extremism of the new government, especially its exclusionary ideology. Ideology was not a huge factor in the pragmatic (though murderous) Marcos government; at the other extreme, the indiscriminate hatreds of the Nazis led to the vast massacres of the Holocaust.

Crisis Genocide

Crisis genocide is brought about or exacerbated by war, either international or civil. Very minor local rebellions can serve as excuses for already-planned and continuing genocide, as in Guatemala in the 1980s up to the present (Nelson 2019). International war can vastly escalate already-ongoing genocides, as in Hitler's Germany in the 1940s. Sometimes consolidation and crisis genocides occur together, as in Cambodia in the late 1970s and Rwanda in 1994, producing the most extreme of all genocides. Almost all genocides fall into one of these three types. The only exceptions are cases in which an extreme (if not actually psychopathic) dictator continues to kill whole populations without ceasing. The Stalin regime is the main modern example.

IMPACT OF GENOCIDE

Almost all genocides fall into one of these types. The only exceptions are cases in which an extreme dictator continues to kill whole populations over many years, even in stable times; the USSR under Stalin is almost the only case. Genocides range greatly in the numbers and percentages of people killed. The Cambodian genocide, which killed 25 percent of the total population, is unique. Rwanda's genocide killed 5 percent of the population—at least half a million people—in only 100 days, a rate of killing that may at times have reached 333.3 murders per hour, 5.5 per minute (Nyseth Brehm 2017b:5; the oft-quoted figure of a million dead is inflated; see Guichaoua 2020 and related articles in *Journal of Genocide Research*, vol. 22, no. 1). Most genocides are fortunately smaller; many are "politicides," confined to classes of political enemies of the dictator. Individual political killings do not count as genocides, but mass political murders by dictators like Pinochet of Chile and Marcos of the Philippines were genocides. They killed not only political opponents but families of opponents, ordinary protestors, children who seemed somehow opposed to the regime, and random suspects.

The scope of genocide depends on the size and range of targeted groups, which in turn depends on the extremism of the exclusionary ideology of the leaders. Hitler targeted a huge and, at the end, almost random-looking assortment of peoples. Pinochet narrowly targeted suspected liberals and leftists. A genocidal leader picks groups already demonized or ostracized by society, or—especially—by the dominant majority of society. Genocidal dictators seek to lead the disenfranchised into attacking successful but politically weak groups, such as the Jews in Hitler's Germany. Hitler targeted all groups that could be seen as a threat to the lives, incomes, or social sensibilities of the German masses. Trump followed him (Neuborne 2019) by inciting his white American base against minorities, educated people (especially women), Jews, Muslims, liberals, gun control advocates, environmentalists, immigrants, the poor, African Americans, and any others who could be perceived as threatening the dominance of white conservatives, especially males.

COMPLICITY

Genocidal actions depend upon finding a base who will support the dictator. Mao Zedong said, "A spark can ignite a prairie fire," but that depends on the availability of dry grass. Threatened persons can easily turn to defensiveness and hatred. The dictator seeks to give credence and voice to their discontent. This involves working back from the ultimate genocide to back stories of angry and disenfranchised populations. The casual tendency of modern historians and other scholars to attribute genocide to causal historical events, such as "the economy," "politics," "culture," or "climate" is simply wrong. Marx is often blamed for this tendency, because of vulgarization of his theory of history, but he was careful to specify that ordinary people must join and believe in revolution for it to occur, even if it is "inevitable" sooner or later because of economic forces. Marx was also aware that those economic forces were themselves caused by the choices of nations and people. Other thinkers from Ibn Khaldun to Max Weber and Anthony Giddens (1984) have made the same general point: structures emerge from individual actions and interactions.

Animal models, of which there are many (Clutton-Brock 2016), suggest that competition for control of resources and of mates and mating bring out the worst in all mammal species, turning otherwise meek and inoffensive animals into demons. Rage over shakiness of control certainly lies behind complicity with genocide and genocidal behavior. Exploring the full scale of this phenomenon, and of other causes for rage, remains an urgent task for the future.

The universality of the phenomenon, especially perhaps in street gangs, suggests that it is all too normal a part of human potential, but many cases chronicled by Weisband (2017), such as the Nazi death camp leaders, seem to be genuinely psychotic or brain damaged. Whatever the explanations, the performative sadism of human violence is a particularly horrific thing to find so universally.

Recent attacks on "social media" as platforms that amplify hatred (e.g., Zaki 2019:146–150) has made us aware of an important and previously neglected fact: the greatest genocides, the ones in which whole nations seem to have gone mad and collapsed in orgies of blood, were propagated by print media and radio. The Turkish massacres of the Armenians and other Christian minorities were prior to radio, but genocides since—notably Germany and central Europe under Hitler; the USSR under Stalin; China under Mao; Nigeria in the Biafra War; and the Indonesian, Cambodian, and Rwanda-Burundi genocides—were driven by newspapers, radio, and public appearances. The worst recent genocide in terms of mass participation by ordinary people is Burma, where access to modern media is limited. The real value of Facebook, Twitter, and other forms of interactive media is that they allow us to answer back, to avoid passivizing and alienating. It allows discussion, persuasion, and mobilization of grassroots movements.

SUMMARY

Ethnic genocide is a relatively new form of evil. Outside of religious persecutions, huge-scale elimination of vast numbers of peaceable fellow citizens, simply because they fall in some arbitrary category, is new enough that people have not adjusted to it as a matter of ordinary life. It has not been with us since time immemorial, as slavery was considered to be. Conforming to genociders is, or was in the early twentieth century, a new way to be evil. The Enlightenment gave rise to ideas of peace and freedom. War was reduced, and slavery slowly but slowly was outlawed everywhere. However, the Enlightenment was founded not only on rapid expansion of trade, commerce, communication, and science, but also on slavery and exploitation. The Enlightenment came to fight these, because well-meaning individuals had to confront the mass horrors of capitalist expansion in the eighteenth and nineteenth centuries.

As population exploded in the twentieth century, pressure on resources and competition for power became more salient. Leaders by this time tended to be elderly and not battle-hardened, so they did not always deal with such problems by international war, as almost everyone had done before 1800. Often, either during war or instead of war, the modern leaders turned on sectors of their own people, waging genocidal campaigns. Wars and slaving were partially replaced by internal mass murder. The origins of genocide lay in religious persecution and settler colonialist practices. It called for mass hatred to provoke support for mass murder. Hateful, disenfranchised, and angry people are susceptible to this persuasion. By mobilizing an insecure or downward-mobile majority, or fraction of the majority, against targeted or disliked minorities, complicity to the dictator results. Citizen participants say they are "following orders" and "doing their job," becoming callous to the whole enterprise (Paxton 2004; Snyder 2015). Like war, genocide is often expressed with seizing loot and land (Kiernan 2007). Like intimate partner violence, it involves control and insecurity about control and power. Like civil war, it often begins with rebellion, driven by class, religious, or ethnic conflict. Finally, the potential of genocide gives credence and social support for the antisocial and destructive genocidal dictators who manifest classic bully behavior. Genocide is a very different phenomenon from civil war and its collateral causalities, as discussed in chapter 2.

NOTES

The nature and promotion of good have been addressed by every religious writer in history, as well as countless psychologists and other scientists. Covering this literature is neither necessary nor possible here. Evil is less well studied. Outside of religious imprecations against sin, there are rather few studies, mostly by psychologists. Of these, particularly valuable are Roy Baumeister's *Evil* (1997), Aaron Beck's *Prisoners of Hate* (1999), Alan Fiske and Taj Rai's *Virtuous Violence* (2014), Ervin Staub's books (1989, 2003, 2011), the Sternbergs' *The Nature of Hate* (2008), and James Waller's *Becoming Evil* (2002) and *Confronting Evil* (2016). Simon Baron-Cohen's *Zero Degrees of Empathy* (2011), Steven Bartlett's *The Pathology of Man* (2005), Gavin de Becker's *The Gift of Fear* (1997), Ben Kiernan's *Blood and Soil* (2007), Robert Sapolsky's *Behave* (2017), and Kathleen Taylor's *Cruelty* (2009) cover some important psychological terrain. Zeki and Romaya (2008) review the physiology of hate. Albert Bandura's book *Moral Disengagement* (2016) exhaustively treats that aspect of evil. Most of these books, as well as the literature on genocide, spice up their texts with horrific stories. Baumeister is especially graphic.

By evil, we mean deliberate harm to people simply because one wants to harm them, because of what they are or might be. It is the state described by words like "murderous," "malevolent," and "cruel." Ordinary selfishness is bad enough, but it is part of the human condition; most of us give ourselves the benefit of the doubt. This is no doubt deplorable most of the time, but it is not what we are considering in this book. E. N. Anderson has devoted two previous books (Anderson 2010, 2014) to the problem of narrow, short-term planning and action. Selfishness can become more evil as it moves into violent robbery, gangsterism, raiding, and onward into outright invasion and aggressive war.

Similarly, violence in defense of self and loved ones is not evil, and is often praiseworthy, but it grades via "preemptive strikes" into aggressive war based on paranoid fears of attack, or on trivial border raids taken as "deadly attacks on the homeland." A transition zone exists between socially sanctioned violence, for example, resisting Hitler in 1941, and excessive use of force, for example, police gunning down an unarmed boy and claiming "defense." Transition zones make moral decisions difficult.

Chapter 2

War and Mass Killing

FORMS OF WAR AND MASS KILLING

War and/or mass killing may include international war, civil war (Collier and Sambanis 2005), revolution and rebellion, genocide, structural violence on large scales, mass poisoning by pollution, denial of medical care, and mass starvation through refusing to take action on agricultural support and food security. Famine has been manipulated for mass murder, as described in harrowing detail in Rhoda Howard-Hassmann's book *State Food Crimes* (2016). Famine in the modern world always involves politics—at best, neglect; at worst, malevolence (Sen 1982). Large-scale ritual human sacrifice, once a major part of religion and kingship, has fortunately been eliminated, but sacrificing millions to the cults of guns, automobiles, and oil continues.

These forms have different causes. International war is hard to predict and almost always multicausal, including desire to capture a neighbor's territory and resources, support of one's own military machine and/or armaments industry, pressure by hot-headed males hungry for glory and loot, claims of wounded national pride, and ideological differences with the enemy. Traditional or manufactured hatreds are conspicuous and small incidents are typically used as excuses. The War of Jenkins' Ear (1739–1748) was not just about Jenkins' ear. It was a complex fight between Britain and Spain over control of New World territories. Medieval Turks and Mongols sometimes had war as their major economic activity and even their whole lifeway. Rivalries within families forced rivals to compete for loot and glory (Fletcher 1980).

Kissel and Kim (2018) define war as an organized conflict between separate, independent groups. They note that the terms "aggression" and "war" cover a vast range of different behaviors and include both insects and mammals, including humans. The genetics of aggression are ambiguous. While "coalitionary" killing of enemies is largely confined to ants, chimpanzees, and humans, only humans do it on a grand scale. The authors point to examples of cannibalism, possibly during famines and archaeological massacres, including one in Kenya 10,000 years ago. They describe a behavioral and cultural shift in war after the development of settled agriculture, but mostly in the scope and organization of war rather than in the frequency of aggressive killing (Kissel and Kim 2018).

War has been around for millennia, if one counts the local raids and small wars typical of small-scale societies, chiefdoms, and early states (Turchin 2006, 2016). Violence is probably as prevalent now as throughout most of history (Mann 2018). Population growth, rivalry for land and loot, and hierarchic institutions have outpaced peacekeeping. Typically, neighboring territories come into conflict over land and resources, but such conflicts can almost always be settled by negotiation. When they get out of control, traditional rivalries may develop, as between France and England through much of history. Then, honor, nationalism, and hatred come into play, increasing the danger. Specific histories are invariably complex and highly contingent on hard-to-predict events.

Human societies are easily persuaded to make war on weaker groups, and only slightly less easily persuaded to gang up on strong groups. The human tendency is to unite against enemies. Humans also opt for available solutions in preference to developing new and untried ones. Massacring the Jews was all too available as a solution for Europeans in the twentieth century; it had been done hundreds of times over hundreds of years, on a small scale, and Jews had been subjected to all sorts of discriminatory rules. Murder was easily scaled up to the Holocaust. Massacring populations in a land grab has a time-honored and culturally available tradition to settlers. Persuading humans to unite behind new and reasonable solutions without eliminating the competition is difficult.

A recent study of war and mass killing by Dean Falk and Charles Hildebolt (2017) describes a wide range of war, mass killings, and violent behavior, from small-scale societies that have essentially no violent killings to those in which a large percentage of the deaths occur from violence. In state-level societies, maintenance of order developed slowly with wide variance among tribal and early state societies. There are violently aggressive, bloodthirsty people and serene, pacific groups.

In few societies are war and mass killing the norm; such a society would quickly self-destruct. However, there are records of a few societies that did so. Something very close to extermination occurred among the Waorani of South America, until they were persuaded by missionaries to become more peaceful (Robarcheck 1989; Robarchek and Robarchek 1998). Historically, there is a range of war and killing in states from Afghanistan and ancient Assyria to relatively peaceful Tokugawa Japan and Yi Korea, or, today, Scandinavia and Switzerland. Most states through history have been undemocratic and repressive, with many political murders. Some mountain refuge areas are notoriously violent: the Caucasus, highland New Guinea, the Afghanistan-Pakistan border. Others are peaceful. Sea raiders are famously murderous, but often become peaceable quite rapidly, as the "sea peoples" of the old Mediterranean appear to have done and the Vikings more recently did. Pastoral tribes are frequently fighters, from the Mongol and Turkic hordes to the Plains tribes of America.

Among the Enga, one of the most violent societies in Falk and Hildebolt's sample mentioned above, powerful self-made leaders—"big men"—often whip up war for their own advantage, but may also make peace for the same reason; the oscillation from peace to extreme violence that has characterized Enga society is heavily determined by these self-aggrandizing maneuvers (Wiessner 2019). Popular will often forces peace on disruptive young men or would-be leaders, however. Most societies swing back and forth between war and peace, conflict and stability, from Melanesia to urban America's less privileged neighborhoods.

Particularly interesting are profound changes over time within population groups. Scandinavians changed from being highly aggressive Vikings to a democratic socialist society (Pinker 2011). The English changed from Shakespeare's blood-drenched warriors to today's peaceable citizenry. Germany changed from one of the most violent countries in history to a leader of peaceful Europe in one generation. Most dramatic was Rwanda, where gradual increase in hate and violence between Tutsis and Hutus built up to the genocide of 1994, killing almost one-tenth of the population. It ended suddenly, followed by a relatively peaceful, tranquil, well-regulated recovery, as shown by our brief research and more detailed ongoing research by Hollie Nyseth Brehm (2020). Violence, however, between Tutsi and Hutus continues unabated in neighboring Democratic Republic of the Congo.

EXEMPLARS OF SOCIAL PHENOMENA EMBRACING MASS KILLING

In this section, we will discuss empire cycles, civil war, slavery, and structural violence.

Empire Cycles

Every preindustrial state has had cycles of rise and fall, usually at vaguely predictable intervals (a 75–100-year period and a 200–300-year cycle being common; Turchin and Zefedov 2009). The great Medieval Arab thinker Ibn Khaldun (1958) first isolated, described, and explained these cycles. Recently, Peter Turchin and collaborators (2003, 2006, 2016; Turchin and Zefedov 2009; E. N. Anderson 2019) have elaborated on Ibn Khaldun's theory. They observe that dynasties, or equivalent powers, take over by military victory. These conquerors often come from the margins of the polity; they are Ibn Khaldun's "barbarians," now termed "semi-peripheral marcher states." They then rise to glory, after which they become corrupt, the economy fails to grow, and expanding populations compete for limited resources. The elites also make war but as wealth ceases to grow, they find it harder to conquer and hold territory outside their limits. Rebellion, local wars, banditry, and sometimes international wars break out as societies dissolve into chaos. A society that starts with a positive-sum game (cooperation, law-abiding) dissolves into negative-sum game in which groups and power brokers try to destroy each other, for example, China's dynastic cycles (Anderson 2019). Richard Lachmann (2020) has elaborated a similar point: elites get sclerotic, the economy stops expanding, and the nation faces a resulting zero-sum game. On rare occasions, a whole empire may completely collapse, as Rome did in the fifth century,

Civil War

Today, a range of violent engagements are common. International war is still with us, although current ones grow mostly from local civil wars. Civil wars abound and merge with local rebellions. Civil wars stem from rebellion, revolution, or coup, or often from breakaway movements by local regions, such as the Civil War in the United States (Collier and Sambanis 2005).

The success of civil war is grounded in disseminating falsehood. Lies are universal in war: "the first casualty, when war comes, is truth" (as Hiram Johnson said during World War I), and George Orwell's analyses in *1984* remain unsurpassed (1950). People believe lies against all evidence when their political beliefs are reinforced, as several modern studies have shown (Healy 2018). Patiently pointing to facts can work, but only when the truth is inescapable and unequivocal (Healy 2018). The endless circulation of repeatedly discredited fictions about Jews and blacks is well known. The "Protocols of the Elders of Zion," shown 100 years ago to be a Russian governmental creation, is still circulating worldwide among bigots. The racist ideas of Hitler and his many followers are still very much with us.

Civil war may include the presence of criminal gangs that dominate whole nations. The current governments of Honduras and El Salvador, as of 2020, are closely aligned to their gangs. Both individual and gang aggression are rooted in rivalry, "honor," acquisition of gain, control of women, or hatred of the "other." These motivations blend into gang killings and state control by militias, armies, and governments. There is no clear separation over issues of control. A murder in a gang-dominated country like El Salvador may have individual, gang, militia, and national overtones. Worldwide, the most frequent murders are within the family; next, within the neighborhood. Mass shootings with unknown victims are relatively rare, although much more common in the United States than in most countries.

In the contemporary world, warfare is constant and technologically sophisticated, militarism is on the increase, and dictatorships are becoming common again. Whole societies are becoming militarized. In a special issue of *Current Anthropology*, devoted to this topic, the editors, Hugh Gusterson and Catherine Besteman (2019), detail the rapid rise and current pervasiveness of the new high-tech militaristic world and worldview. Military bases around the world have led to virtual slavery of local hired workers, as well as dispossession of local farmers and others (Lutz 2019; Vine 2019). Besteman's article (2019) details the progressive conversion of the world into an armed camp, with the rich routinely attacking poor nations—not a new phenomenon—but now with a worldwide, unified effort, rather than a country-by-country attempt. Gusterson (2019) recounts the use of drones to create terror; there is no one to fight—only a strange, buzzing object that brings random death and chaos. As Gusterson shows, drones are claimed to hit actual individual terrorists and military targets with pinpoint accuracy, but, of course, they do no such thing. They terrorize whole populations with large-scale random strikes on soft targets. Militarized cultures develop in zones of war and conflict, as they have throughout time (Fattal 2019; Hammami 2019).

Several recent studies attempt to quantify deaths by violence in human societies. Stephen Pinker (2011) concludes people kill much less in recent times than previously. Douglas Fry (2013) and Michael Mann (2018) disagree, though stating that small-scale societies do often kill at a relatively high rate; they show that Pinker cherry-picked particularly savage small-scale societies and understated modern killing. Many small-scale farming societies, especially chiefdoms, are particularly bloody. Today, about 1 percent of humans die by violence each year. The incidence varies from almost zero in societies with total peace to a majority of the population dying violently within a year in some extreme war situations of the past. As of 2020, the global average murder rate across the world was 7.6 per 100,000 people, but there is wide variation. For example, Liechtenstein and Monaco report zero murders, Japan and Singapore report 0.2, while El Salvador reports 82.8, Honduras reports 56.5, and the U.S. Virgin Islands reports 49.3 (www. https ://worldpopulationreview.com/countries/murder-rate-by-country/ retrieved April 7, 2020).

Slavery

Slavery is another example of mass killing. It continues currently in some areas around the world. Mistreatment of enslaved people involves minimalizing them—not denying their humanity, but denying that it matters. They can be treated brutally because they do not count. It is perhaps harder to imagine the mindsets of people who worked in the slave trade, day after day, for a whole working lifetime, than to imagine the mindsets of genociders. Today, most people in developed countries are repelled even by bad treatment of farm animals. We remember when people treated animals worse than they do today, but even in our natal rural environments, animals were never treated as badly as slaves were treated in Zanzibar, Byzantium, the American South, and many other places. The animals needed to stay healthy to turn a profit. By contrast, the whole goal of slaving is to reduce humans to helpless, terrified victims, through intimidation and brutalization. Their health was a secondary concern at best. It was often easier to get new slaves than to deal with well-treated ones.

At the slave museum in Zanzibar, created from the old slave quarters there, we witnessed the hellholes where slaves were confined, read their stories, and saw excellent exhibits with contemporary accounts, drawings, and photographs. The most disquieting, and the most pervasive, message is that the slave trade was an ordinary business, like selling bananas. Hundreds of people routinely raped, murdered, tortured, brutalized, and oppressed their fellow humans, for 8 hours a day or more, simply as a regular job. These slavers no doubt felt like any other workers—bored, annoyed by trivial problems, angry at the boss every so often, but indifferent to the subjects of their effort. They were not particularly violent, or psychopathic, or intolerant; they were simply locals who happened to be available. Anyone could do it.

Slavery has cast a long shadow over the world, especially the Caribbean and the United States. The history of slavery in the United States profoundly influences American politics to this day (Acharya et al. 2018). Many white Americans believe slavery was a happy state of being where blacks played banjos and occasionally picked a bit of cotton under the benevolent eyes of the plantation owners. The rest usually think of slavery as the work of a few utterly evil men, like Simon Legree of *Uncle Tom's Cabin*. The fact is that slavery involved thousands of men and women brutalizing other men and women, simply as a regular job, carried out with varying degrees of racist hate but with little thought about the whole issue. In America the brutalizers were white and the victims black, but in most of history—and today in countries like Thailand and Ukraine—the slaves were often of the same race and very often from the same culture and society as their oppressors. Roy Baumeister, in his book *Evil* (1997), comments on how repugnant most people find evil acts, but how quickly they get used to them and see them as routine. There is no evidence that slavers found even the initial phases of their work particularly unpleasant.

John Stedman wrote a classic eighteenth-century account of the horrors of slavery in Surinam (Stedman 1988 [1790]). Stedman was a mercenary in the service of the plantation owners, so, at first, he was biased in favor of slavery and against slaves. His horror at what he saw convinced him that slavery was an evil practice. He reports a great deal of real hatred by slaveowners toward their slaves, but a great deal more simple indifference, including torture simply for torture's sake. There was extreme fear of slave rebellions, and the fear-driven belief that only brutality could prevent those. His writings became foundational to the antislavery effort, first in England, then worldwide. Most interesting, though, is his extremely extensive documentation of everyday brutality. It simply never occurred to people of the time that this was monstrous.

One also recalls John Newton's conversion, at about the same time, from slaving captain to extremely repentant Christian; after years of depression, he felt divine forgiveness, and wrote the hymn "Amazing Grace," which, somewhat ironically, became a favorite of African American churches. As with resisters of pressure to commit genocide, repenters of slaving are rare in the archives.

Slavery in traditional societies (from the Northwest Coast of North America to pre-slave-trade Africa) was sometimes less murderous and torture-filled. But it was never other than cruel and oppressive. All records from all societies speak of rape, terrorizing, and brutalizing. Yet, almost no one in history opposed slavery as an institution, until the Quakers in the eighteenth century concluded it was against God's law. The tide then turned with striking speed. Enslavement of Europeans was basically over, outside the Turkish Empire, well before 1800. A few local sects banned slavery among their faithful even in the ancient world, and Islam nominally banned—but did not effectively stop—enslaving other Muslims (Graeber 2014). Slavery went on, never opposed by any significant movement. Enslavement of Native Americans was theoretically banned in the Catholic countries, and was actually reduced to a rare and local phenomenon by 1800. Enslavement of Africans continued well into the nineteenth century, being legally abolished in country after country between 1820 and the 1880s.

Illegal slavery continues today (Fein 2007). The Council on Foreign Relations (2019) estimates that there are 40.3 million slaves in the world. Some are domestic slaves like those in Saudi Arabia. Most are forced prison laborers (e.g., in North Korea), persons enslaved for debt, or sex slaves (including those in forced marriages). Sex slavery, with all the attendant horrors, is carried out in the familiar spirit of "all in a day's work," by thugs and pimps from Thailand to Hollywood. Reading reports of child sex slavery shows how low humans can sink, all the time thinking they are doing what culture and economics require (see, for example, Fein 2007). As in other slaveries, there is no evidence that most of these people are especially evil to begin with. Some child sex slavers are clearly psychopathic, but others simply drift into the life. Some had been victims themselves. Slavery is an outcrop of war, mass killing, and structural violence.

Structural Violence

Millions of deaths today are the result of structural violence and injustice against people, bureaucratic attitudes that categorize people are merely things to move around, like rocks. One of the most chilling books is *The Future of Large Dams* by Thayer Scudder (2005). Scudder spent his life studying refugees from huge dam projects. In almost every case, people displaced by big dams were simply ordered to move. Their homes were bulldozed, their livelihoods flooded. There were usually token "relief" efforts, but these were so trivial as to be more insulting than helpful. Millions of refugees were left to shift for themselves, and in poorer nations that meant many or most of them died of starvation, exposure, or illnesses. Scudder bends over backward to be fair, which makes the stories sound even worse; one cannot write him off as biased. The bureaucrat perpetrators are cut from the same cloth as the "doing my job" slavers and Nazi executioners. There is a huge subsequent literature on dams and displacement. Suffice it to cite Sunil Amrith's *Unruly Waters* (2018), which puts India's and China's mega-dams in historical context while describing their social and ecological devastation. Almost always, the displaced are poor, and often from minority groups, while the benefits go to the rich. Environmental injustice includes pollution generated by giant firms producing for the affluent, but this pollution is almost always dumped on the poor and vulnerable (E. N. Anderson 2010 covers this issue in detail). The populations sacrificed for the greater good of the giant firms are the stigmatized ones. Erving Goffman's classic work *Stigma* (1963) is highly relevant. Likewise, is lack of access to health care and institutional violence against specific populations, for example, poor and marginalized childbearing women in America (B. Anderson and L. Roberts 2019).

Related are the horrific famines invoked by governments against their own people, as described in *State Food Crimes* (Howard-Hassmann 2016; see also Sen 1982). Specific, particularly horrible, cases are covered by Anne Appelbaum (2017) for Ukraine in the 1930s and Hazel Cameron (2018) for Zimbabwe in 1984. Not only totalitarian governments, but the British in Ireland (1846–1849) and Bengal (1942–1943), callously allowed famine to occur. Most settler societies have done the same in their campaigns to get rid of colonized peoples. In the Irish potato famine, aid was denied although Ireland was exporting food and England was rich (Salaman 1985; Woodham-Smith 1962). Many countries have deliberately invoked famine as a form of state policy. The Holodomor in the Ukraine and Russia in the 1920s was an extreme case (Howard-Hassmann 2016). America's nineteenth-century extermination of the buffalo, a genocidal act, was explicitly done to starve the Native Americans.

Johan Galtung (1969) coined the term "structural violence" to describe destruction by the cold workings of the social system, ranging from the results of institutionalized bigotry to bureaucratic displacement and refusal to provide famine relief. Structural violence is usually a matter of passing public costs onto those held to deserve no better, usually poor and vulnerable people. Again, ethnic and religious hate is very often involved. The targeted victims—selected to pay the costs of industrial development, public works, crop failures, dysfunctional health care systems, and the like—are almost always poor, and very often from minority groups.

There is, however, a range from clearly and deliberately murderous and unnecessary structural violence, such as the Holodomor and the Ethiopian famine under the Dergue (Dikötter 2019), which is clearly genocide, down to the tragic results of incompetent and irresponsible planning. Famines before 1900 were usually due to genuine crop failures in societies that did not have adequate safety nets, and often could not have had. The gradation from such tragedies to deliberate mass murder by starvation is not an easy one to unpack. There will always be controversial cases. Lillian Li's classic *Fighting Famine in North China* (2007) goes into detail on a society that was desperately short of food but did have a well-developed safety net; the famines reflected a complex interaction of crop failures, local violence, and government success or failure at deploying their extensive but shaky relief infrastructure. Such cases remain outside the scope of this book, which deals only with cases such as the Holodomor and the North American buffalo slaughter, in which famine was deliberately created for genocidal reasons. Selective removal of whole ethnic groups for bureaucratic projects, as in Stalin's USSR, is also genocidal.

Thus, ordinary callousness toward the unfortunate can grade into genocide, often quite insidiously. The problem is usually one of causing enormous costs to people who "don't count" in order to provide often-slight benefits for the ones who "do count." This used to be common in declining empires, but now is the prerogative of dinosaur productive interests, above all the fossil fuel industry, as well as big dams and other public projects. The dams notoriously provide electricity for urban elites and irrigation water for agribusiness while displacing whole populations of nonaffluent local people. Somewhat similar is the case of those who price gouge for necessities, notably the giant pharmaceutical firms. We hereby introduce the word "bureaupathy" to describe this associated attitude and mindset. It is quite different from greed; the bureaucrats are usually following orders or truckling to rich clients, rather than enriching themselves.

Another form of structural violence is the systematic bigotry characterizing ethnic relations between majorities and minorities in many nations, from China and Myanmar to Brazil and the United States. American minorities, especially but not only African Americans and Native Americans, are subjected not only to discriminatory behavior but to unpunished murders by police and vigilantes, and to health care disparities so extreme as to count as murder by malign neglect. Ongoing systemic bigotry has been a presage to genocide in many cases, including settler genocide of Native Americans in the United States, as well as the Nazi genocides and the Rwandan massacres. Over many centuries, structural violence through discriminatory behavior has killed vast numbers of people, often wiping out entire minority communities.

MASS KILLING AND HATRED

Hatred causes genuinely gratuitous harm: no one benefits. In fact, the hater usually harms himself or herself just to hurt others; suicide bombing is the purest case. Hatred is a negative-sum game: both sides lose. This negative-sum gaming is currently destroying world social orders. Suicide bombers and suicidal mass shooters are the true emblematic figures of the twenty-first century. On a wider scale, the suicidal environmental ruin of the environment by fossil fuel and other destructive corporations is the same. The high administrators of those corporations know they will be dead before the real costs of fossil fuels come in to destroy many lives, but from the viewpoint of entire countries and populations, it is suicide bombing writ large. Similarly, crushing African Americans in the United States is pure cost to society; millions of people with high potential are prevented from realizing that potential, while their oppressors—far from benefiting—lose the valuable contributions those millions might have made. Moreover (to return to a point made by John Stedman, and by many since) oppressing people costs the oppressor, who devotes most of his life to fear and cruelty.

Selfish greed, however, does benefit the doer; it harms the other people in the transaction while benefiting the perpetrator. Big dams benefit the rich and urban, but usually hurt the displaced people and the total economy. The cost-benefit ratios of big dams are notoriously bad (Scudder 2005). More pure cases of selfish greed, such as drug gang violence and medieval Viking raids, are even clearer: the thugs get some loot, but the entire polity suffers, especially but not only the looted victims. Professional gambling is another case in point: the house always wins in the end, since it is there to make a profit. Casino owners get rich. They do it at the expense of victims, often nonafflu- ent and often compulsive, who are ruined and frequently commit suicide. The total cost-benefit ratio is negative. But the victims choose to gamble, so it is hard to stop the industry. In this case, as in "the right to bear arms" and many others, individual liberty is traded off against social costs.

Wars to acquire land and mineral resources, to help one's national arma- ments industry, and to support its military, are universal throughout history. Group hatred remains a strategy. The deadly mix of social fear, social hate, and need for social control is the real "heart of darkness" within humans. Far more dangerous are issues of power and control. Gavin de Becker (1997) provided many accounts of psychopaths and mass murderers. All turn on the obsessive need of the killer to control someone—the woman he is stalking, the parents who have tortured him growing up, the owner of a valued good who has tried to protect it.

Killers in such situations may commit suicide or be easily caught, but those who kill randomly or who target homeless or otherwise "marginal" people may not be. Many gangs require a new recruit to commit a murder, as a rite of passage. Such initiates seek out homeless mentally ill individuals who will not be missed (or even identified, in many cases) and whose death will not be investigated seriously. This murder for position leads to further crime. In the United States such killers are usually jailed eventually, but they rarely are in much of Latin America.

In war and mass killing, the outcome is clear-cut. However, much killing, based on greed and control is more silent, for example, promotion of tobacco, dumping pollution in poverty neighborhoods, displacing populations through large dams, denying essential care to disenfranchised childbearing women. The role of hate in such callous situations cannot be underestimated. Several recent studies attempt to quantify deaths by violence in human societies. Since death is forever, the consequences of murder are irreparable, while good is eas- ily undone A society requires countless small good acts to make up for a termi- nally bad one. Society must leverage the positive to keep societies functional.

SUMMARY

The ability of people to change dramatically from war mode to peace mode, from bad wolf to good wolf, is truly astounding. Recent studies have shown that this is heavily contingent upon social pressure. In an experimental game, Michal Bauer and coworkers (2018) found that Slavic-origin high school stu- dents in Slovakia were twice as likely to display hostility toward Roma than toward other Slavic students, but only if someone started it. They would all play peacefully unless someone made a hostile move. If that happened, the Slavic students generally joined in. It was easy to flip the group from tolerant to ethnically discriminatory. Chapter 3 explores the issues of social pressure, conformity, complicity, and the individual and collection actions that march toward genocide.

Chapter 3

Conformity and Complicity

KILLING UNDER PRESSURE

One fact is common in all genocides and wars: An individual or a few individuals whip up hatred, and the public goes along. Usually, leaders are desperate for power and are not particularly restrained by morals. The masses, however, can be almost anyone, anywhere, anytime, although most sources agree that genuinely threatening and unsettled conditions make it easier for tyrants to raise enmity. Hate is the starting point. Without hatred, no dictator can hold place, let alone start a genocide. The dictator may be cold, calculating, and hate-driven. The masses who support him must have that hatred instilled or mobilized. The bad wolf must be fed, starving the good wolf. Ordinary people must be coerced from their normal, peaceful state to a destructive state where hatred dominates.

Occasionally there are mobs that spontaneously riot and destroy minority neighborhoods, but even these normally have a single instigator or small group of instigators. Sometimes, ongoing conflict with horrific levels of violence lasts for decades. A particularly thorough and revealing study of violence in such situations is Wolfgang Gabbert's study of the Yucatan "caste war" from 1848 to 1901, as described in *Violence and the Caste War of Yucatan* (2019). The rebels developed into the Kruso'ob, "people of the cross," and maintained independence in Quintana Roo for over fifty years. Having lived and worked with descendants of the rebels in Quintana Roo, Mexico, for extended periods over twenty-five years, I (ENA) can testify that these descendants are extremely pleasant and among the most peaceable people I have ever known. Their ancestors, however, were engaged in a long war with no quarter given on either side. This was not genocide—it was an outright war, with approximately evenly matched sides. The amount of mass killing of noncombatants over a fifty-year period was appalling.

On a more daily and mundane level, humans are subject to resentment and frustration that can flip from peace to resentful anger almost instantly. These emotions are the result of ongoing, often invisible tensions that result in the sharp exchanges of daily life. Without peaceful resolution, these outbreaks are food for the bad wolf, enabling the transition to violence. People who appear tranquil may be scared, overly conformist, resentful, or doubting their own abilities to resist in a positive manner. These victims of inanition are the ones most easily duped over time by strongmen and then led to genocidal murder.

The level of change from peaceful to extremely violent can be sudden, overt, and dramatic. Most cultures have some form of the special behavior seen in Scandinavia ("berserker)"; in Malaysia and Indonesia (*mengamok*; "running amuck" is a Western perversion of this phrase); in ancient Ireland ("battle frenzy"); or in the Native Americans of the Plains societies ("crazy dog warriors"). An individual demonstrating this behavior usually does so in battle, but sometimes it occurs in peacetime. The individual snaps, turning into a killing machine, attacking enemies or random bystanders without mercy. This widespread phenomenon indicates how far humans can go in violence. It is a cultural construction or elaboration of the human tendency to "lose it" from extreme rage. It is an expected pattern of behavior under certain circumstances; Celtic and Indonesian warriors in the old days were expected to show this behavior in the heat of battle.

However, most people are relatively inactive during genocide. They may provide moral support and backing, even enthusiastically, or they may be secretly opposed, but generally they do not participate in the killing. This job is left to armies, militias, and police. The exceptions, however, are significant. Mao Zedong, the Khmer Rouge, the Interahamwe in Uganda, and several other genociders mobilized large percentages of the citizenry, turning them into savage killers. On a much smaller but quite significant scale, gangs from the Sicilian Mafia to the drug cartels in Mexico and northern Central America frequently involve many or most of the young male population in certain communities.

This is normally accomplished via social pressure. Charles Anderton and Jurgen Brauer (2019) have provided network explanatory models. Individuals link within their own social networks, parties and forces involved link along their wider ones, and media provides wide saturation. The authors stress the importance of radios, estimating that government radio programs explained about 10 percent of the Rwanda genocide. They summarize several possibilities for mobilization. Whole regions may suddenly flip, or one area may while another does not. Individuals may flip from perpetrator to rescuer, as did

Oskar Schindler (see Thomas Keneally's 1982 account in *Schindler's List*). Likewise, the rescuer may become the perpetrator, or even *"rescuer and perpetrator at the same time"* (Anderton and Bauer 2019:482, their emphasis). Changes can be sudden, and individuals frequently experience remorse after the killing.

Genocide leaders are geniuses at facilitating this psychological transition, motivated by extremist views, extreme hatred, and power-seeking. They have charisma, often creating cults of personality. They can manipulate social fear, using a mix of charisma and exaggerated group rivalry. They can whip up any hatred—latent, traditional, or salient. They are masters of redefining groups, taking advantage of cleavage lines, to make them smaller, tighter, more defensive, more closed, circling the wagons. They can spin the message as a "state of exception" (Agamben 2004) when moral rules are broken to harm a rival group (Sapolsky 2017:674). People become more sensitive to ominous messages, less sensitive to rational considerations, and blinded by rage (Monbiot 2019). A narcissistic, cocksure, extremist leader can manage to take advantage of human loyalty, religion, or ideology to reduce a whole nation to near-hypnotism, adulating him with worshipful adoration.

Frank Dikötter (2019) has investigated this with several twentieth-century dictators, including Mussolini, Hitler, and Stalin, finding common threads. All of these dictators consolidated power ruthlessly and depended upon a cult of personality. They became strongmen, above the law, above tradition, above any restraint—even the restraints of their own alleged ideologies. The more ruthless they became, the more their base adored them, until they miscalculated and caused actual ruin through war or economic collapse. The tendency of humans to conform with society and its leaders—usually a useful trait, preventing chaos—can be misused. People then vote or act out, following their worst emotions to follow their worst leaders.

Their followers, at first, are usually thugs, rebels, toughs. The circle of followers usually expands slowly to include everyday racists and bigots. Mussolini's Fascists and Hitler's Nazis remained small but highly visible and violent groups for over a decade before taking over Italy and Germany. The same was true of groups as disparate as Lenin's Bolsheviks and the early Interahamwe of Rwanda. With a charismatic leader, the circle of followers eventually expands to include quiet, peaceful but resentful citizens. To the degree that they are weak and easily led, they are swayed by rhetoric and by the pressure of mass mobilization. Dramatically rapid mobilization of hate and violence occurred, for example, in Rwanda and Serbia, mobilizing latent hatreds.

Mass conformity is extensively documented. It builds upon traditional hatreds, for example, as against Jews in "Christian" Europe. Ordinary people almost always conform (Baumeister 1997; Waller 2016). The vast majority of killing and harming in this world is done by people just doing their job, as demonstrated in Roy Baumeister's 1997 book *Evil: Inside Human Violence and Cruelty*. Genociders, bandit gangs, slave traders, bureaucrats refusing food aid, and others are not insane or sadistic killers, at least not initially. Most report hating their work and being repelled by it at first, but habituating to it quite soon. The degree to which ordinary people can change rapidly from one state to another, regardless of ideology, personality, and religion, is the subject of analysis in a recent book (Newman 2020). In a genocidal meltdown, almost everyone becomes either a perpetrator or sympathizer. This current work builds upon previous work by Newman and Erber (2002) examining a comprehensive psychological and social model of these roles. (Additional recent reviews are found in Paxton 2005, Snyder 2015, Staub 2011, Tatz and Higgins 2016, and Waller 2016.)

People are swept away by rhetoric and then strengthened in murderous resolve by the fact that everyone else is involved in the killing. Most people simply do what they were told or what their neighbors are doing, simply a job that had to be done. Judging from personal accounts—highly suspect, since generally written for self-exoneration—many seem to have been caught up in the hate; the rest went along out of fear. It is often pointed out that Hitler was proven to kill only one person: himself. He was suspected of earlier murders, but these remain unproved though some at least are fairly certain (Rosenbaum 2014). It was the people "just following orders" that did the real work.

The testimony of many anthropologists (e.g., Atran 2010, 2015), psychologists (Baumeister 1997), criminologists (De Becker 1997), and other experts confirm that perfectly normal people can and do become terrorists and murderers in any social situation that puts a high value on such behavior as serving the group. Scott Atran (2010) found Islamic terrorists particularly revealing: the terrorists and suicide bombers are usually young persons who have experienced traumatic events in their own small worlds. They are not particularly violent, certainly not psychotic, though they are often resentful. They are often deeply hurt by the killing of their family members or friends. They are very often recruited through intensive influence by leaders of local extremist organizations—leaders who rarely endanger themselves. Accounts of recruits to violent gangs often speak of neighborhoods where the only alternative to membership in a violent gang is being killed by one. Criminals who are not part of gangs are somewhat more apt to be genuinely demented—usually psychopathic—although writers like Roy Baumeister and Gavin De Becker stress that they appear superficially normal. The pirates, smugglers, and killers that ENA knew while doing research on Asian waterfronts seemed to be poor, marginal, and normal waterfront residents caught up in an ugly world with few alternatives. By contrast, the one American mass killer that

ENA knew was a deeply troubled individual, bullied and treated cruelly for his obvious mental health issues until he finally snapped.

There are people whose inner demons drive them out of control, although they can be identified and stopped (De Becker 1997). Far more common are ordinary individuals: "normal" persons with two wolves waiting to be fed. The relevant works are surprisingly silent on what makes one or the other wolf take over in everyday life. The old Victorian clichés—coming from bad seed or a broken home, falling in with bad company, taking to drink—are echoed to this day in one form or another (e.g., by De Becker, and by Alvarez and Bachman in their authoritative text *Violence: The Enduring Problem*, 2017). Virtually anyone can be converted, rather easily, into a monster who will torture, rape, and murder his or her neighbors and even family members for reasons that no rational person could possibly accept after serious consideration. Religious wars over heresies provide extreme cases. In the Albigensian Crusade, the thirteenth-century genocide that gave rise to the famous line "kill 'em all and let God sort 'em out," probably fewer than one in a thousand participants could explain the differences between Catholic and Albigensian Christianity (Anderson and Anderson 2013). Yet the murders of neighbors and friends went on for decades. In the ISIL persecution of Shi'a Muslims, group hate and antagonism are the core issues (Hawley 2018; Wohl et al. 2020) while actual knowledge of the Quran by ISIL members is often fragmentary (Atran 2010).

In most genocides, those who resisted and worked to save victims were astonishingly few. Tatz and Higgins (2016) have recently collected the data from the Holocaust and other genocides. They find that even if there were no penalties for refusing, ordinary people went along with mass murder. This was as true in the United States and Australia in the nineteenth century as in Hitler's Germany and Pol Pot's Cambodia. It is sobering for modern Americans to read how otherwise normal, reasonably decent, "Christian" Americans could perform the most unspeakable acts on Native Americans—often neighbors and (former) friends—without a second thought (Cameron et al. 2015; Madley 2016). Colin Tatz' harrowing summary of settler genocides in Australia reveals the same (Tatz 2018). Nor did more moral citizens do much to restrain the killers. The "Indian lovers" like Helen Hunt Jackson and James Mooney who agitated to protect Native Americans in late nineteenth-century America were few.

Hollie Nyseth Brehm (2017b), in a particularly thorough analysis of the Rwandan genocide, found that killing was clearly top-down directed, with a concentration around the capital and major cities and among well-educated, elite people. It was widespread in regions with low marriage rates, high mobility, concentration of Tutsi, and political opposition—especially by Hutu themselves—at the grassroots. The areas in and around the capital,

Kigali, were far more deadly than areas at the northern margins of the country, partly due to competition for land. This is the opposite of the pattern seen in settler genocides, where murder was far more common on borders where settler populations were expanding at the expense of Indigenous people.

Accounts from China's Cultural Revolution indicate that people were swept up in mass hysteria, but were also afraid to appear neutral, since lack of enthusiasm in persecuting victims led to substantial trouble. An unenthusiastic warrior often became a victim. A few of the many memoirs indicate that the writers were unreconstructed Maoists, but the vast majority worked under orders, from fear or social pressure for conformity. Many repented, and later wrote agonizing stories of their internal sufferings as well as the sufferings they inflicted and endured.

CONFIRMING VULNERABILITY TO PRESSURE

It takes some but not much effort to make people deliberately harm those who have not harmed them. Following discovery of this fact among Nazi survivors, psychologists experimented with students, studying the ease of making students cruel to other students. This is shown in Stanley Milgram's famous experiments with faked electric shocks (1974) and Philip Zimbardo's experiments with students acting as jailers and prisoners (2008). Zimbardo's experiment with a mock prison, at Stanford, had to be stopped within a week, because the students took their roles too seriously. This led to major reforms of experimental ethics, as well as to much soul-searching (Zimbardo 2008). Contrary to published accounts, Zimbardo did not initially allow the "prisoners" to leave the experimental situation. He has faced criticism for this experiment. The privileged white and Asian young men (as these students were) hardly provide a realistic prison situation, given America's racist and brutal prison system (Blum 2018), but this makes the results starker, not less revealing. Critiques by Blum (2018), Haslam et al. (2019), and Le Texier (2019) expose many flaws in the study but do not change the general conclusion. In fact, reanalysis by Reicher, Van Bavel, and Haslam (2020) strengthens the point that people obey authority and may exceed instructions in a negative direction. People become devils very fast, as witnessed in the current U.S. border enforcement by ICE. Zimbardo's main finding stands: people, even the "best" young men, can turn into evildoers with astonishing ease if they are following orders (Zimbardo 2018; Zimbardo and Haney 2020).

There is a continuum, but it phenomenologically feels as if we are dominated by either the good wolf or the bad one—not by an intermediate, neutral wolf. Anger may arise over quite impersonal issues. John Tierney and Roy Baumeister provide an excellent account of this dynamic in their book *The Power of Bad* (2019; see, for example, p. 149). People are often consumed with anger over social issues that may not concern them directly or angered by reading about injustice, murder, or war in far-away places involving strangers. Some people are outraged by the very existence of African Americans, Jews, or Moldavians or by the fact that not everyone worships in their own prescribed way. Ron Rolheiser (2018) writes with some ironic detachment about the human proclivity to moral outrage. Humans love to work themselves up into anger, or even hysteria, about perfectly trivial issues and far-away events irrelevant to their own lives. Most of the evil discussed in Rolheiser's book is deliberately chosen because of outrage over something that does not directly or seriously concern the outraged person. Jews were not really destroying Germany, the Tutsi were not causing much trouble in Rwanda, and the victims of Mao's purges were not engaged in anything worthy of national outrage and mass murder. Most openly expressed hatred is more for what people are as opposed to what they may have done (Gordon Allport 1954). Hannah Arendt's famous phrase "the banality of evil" (Arendt 1963) is compelling. Indeed, evil is banal, for the very good reason that it is usually done by the kid next door, or his equivalent. Arendt describes Eichmann as thoroughly reprehensible, yet he managed to seem chillingly "ordinary" in Germany and in the subsequent war tribunals (Arendt 1963).

Peace came to Colombia after more than fifty years of conflict between the government—often via paramilitary gangs—and FARC, which began as a rebel organization but became largely a cocaine ring. Both groups accommodated to the organized drug cartels. Thousands of people were involved in torture, rape, and murder associated with such activities. With peace came rehabilitation. Anthropologist Sara Reardon (2018) investigated the process. She quotes one of the rehabilitation psychologists, Natalia Trujillo: "I realized not all of them are sociopaths. I realized most of them are also victims" (p. 20). In fact, Reardon describes that the vast majority were closer to victimhood than to pathology. They were local people, some originally idealistic, swept up in a nightmare. Many were forced to fight to save themselves and their families. Most of the combatants returned to ordinary life with varying degrees of success; some have been killed by revengeful persons who were devastated and experienced great losses. Unfortunately, but predictably, the peace did not hold.

Cultural and individual differences do matter. Humans learn from their parents and peers how to cope with direct challenges. As they grow, they must satisfy material needs and exert some control over their universe. This entails managing inevitable fears and challenges. The average human seems easily persuaded to wad up frustrations, threats, and hurts into a ball and throw it at minorities and nonconformists. Projection, displacement, and scapegoating are common themes in all studies of human evil, above all in conforming to genocide.

In times of trouble, the simplest option is to follow the orders of those who appear to know what to do, or to conform with cultural norms that provide strategies for dealing with problems. The next most available option is to maintain a front of hostility—to be touchy, aggressive, or fearful. Ideally, one can seek out the knowledge to cope better, but this requires effort and time. One can simply die, flee, hide, or act as virtuous as possible in the hopes that justice will prevail. Recognizing this choice matrix makes the victory of the bad wolf more understandable. Facing a hostile world, people are prone to let the bad wolf roam, because the other options are too difficult.

The model of conforming to genocide that emerges, then, is one of ordinary people dealing with ordinary stresses, becoming resentful, and easily persuaded by extremist leaders to direct frustration at scapegoats. Social pressure is the direct and immediate cause of the flip to evil, but there is a back story of ordinary human anger and resentment with the minor and major trials of life. Scapegoating minorities by venting diffuse anger is food for the bad wolf. Violence comes from directing diffuse hate to a specific target, usually traditionally devalued groups.

SUMMARY

Violence equals war and genocide when humans, with their own damaged lives, are swayed by evil leaders willing to go beyond normal social rules. This is the strategy of evil leaders from Caligula to Hitler. The immediate cure is minimizing offense-taking and building tolerance, but the ultimate cure is finding good in the world to balance out the offenses—feeding the good wolf. In part I we explored complicity with genocide. In part II we examine the roots of human evil.

NOTE

Dictators in recent decades have always been male. Charismatic yet blood-stained female rulers existed in the past, such as Empress Wu of China and Queen Sorghaqtani of Mongolia. Right-wing and military attitudes toward women have discouraged women from dictatorial positions in recent years, although Mao Zedong's wife Jiang Qing was partly to blame for China's Great Cultural Revolution in the 1960s.

Part II

THE ROOTS OF HUMAN EVIL

"Put in their hands thy bruising irons of wrath,
That they may crush down with heavy fall
The usurping helmets of our adversaries"

William Shakespeare
(*Richard III* Act V, scene 3)

Chapter 4

Human Nature

THEORIES OF HUMAN NATURE

Speculations on human nature have taken place throughout the ages. The classic Christian and Buddhist views are that people everywhere are basically good; evil is a corruption of their nature by bad desires. The problem, according to Buddhist theology, is giving way to greed, anger, and lust or pride, symbolized in Buddhist art by a pig, a dog, and a rooster. The Christian tradition is similar: "love of money is the root of all evil," according to the disciple Paul (I Timothy 10). Most Confucians follow the great Confucian teacher Mencius who viewed people as basically prosocial, unless corrupted by bad or inadequate education (see Mencius, translation by D. C. Lau 1970). Xunzi (1999, orig. third to fourth century BCE) argued this opposite view against Mencius' optimistic view.

Many small-scale and traditional societies claim that people are basically sociable and well-meaning, but must develop themselves through spiritual discipline and cultivation. Quakers speak of the "inner light." Modern biologists and anthropologists have found it in the social and proto-moral inclinations now known to be innate in humans. The highly positive view of humans was especially prevalent in the 1950s–1960s, informed humanistic psychology (Rogers 1961) and launched the self-improvement, New Age, and personal growth industry that peaked in the 1970s. Cold reality withered these movements by the 1990s.

The optimistic view goes back to the ancient Greeks, who wrote of human abilities to love, cooperate, and found democracies. Christianity later built on a view that people could love each other. The line "love thy neighbor as thyself" goes back to Moses. However, few could see humanity as innately good, or believe in virtuous utopias. On the whole, the "noble savage," as

41

described by John Dryden, is largely a straw man. In spite of claims otherwise, Rousseau did not use the phrase and negated the idea. It does not survive the many accounts of war in small-scale societies. Even relatively "noble savage"-believing sources (e.g., Fry 2013) cannot gloss over the frequency of killing in human societies.

Conversely, the most common Western worldview comes from Niccolo Machiavelli, Thomas Hobbes, and Sigmund Freud. This premise is that people are basically evil, selfish, competitive, and out for themselves at the expense of others. This view also goes back to the ancient Greeks, many of whom held that desirable social behavior must be forced upon people by harsh training. Marshall Sahlins (2008) has provided a full history of this sour perspective, showing how widespread it has been in the West and how destructive it has been. Hobbes saw "the life of man in his natural state" as being "solitary, poore, nasty, brutish and short," with people in a permanent condition of "warre of each against all" for resources (Hobbes 1950 [1657]:104). Freud took an even darker view. Innate human nature was the *id*, the realm of terrifying lust, murderous hate, and insatiable greed. Both men thought "savages" showed "man in his natural state." They relied upon romantic travelers' tales rather than real descriptions, and thought "savages" were bloodthirsty, cruel, and driven by the lusts of the moment with no thought of the future. Even in Hobbes' time, before modern anthropology, actual accounts demonstrated that small-scale societies were about as peaceful and orderly as larger societies. The dark view prospered in spite of evidence.

These views come from traditional folk wisdom, which incorporates a good deal of cynicism based on the common observation of people hurting themselves to hurt others more. A worldwide folktale tells of a man who is granted one wish (by an angel, godmother, or some other being) on the condition that his neighbor will get twice what he gets; if the man wishes for a thousand dollars, his neighbor gets two thousand. The man thinks for a while, then says "Make me blind in one eye!". Machiavelli, Hobbes, Freud, and their followers assumed that society must impose powerful discipline to force people to act decently, an impossible task. Joseph Henrich (2016), among many others, has pointed out that only an animal with cumulative culture, natural sociability, and an innate tendency to cooperate could expect conformity to social norms. Voorhees et al. agree "the evolution of human cooperative behavior required . . . the cultural formation of kinship-based social organizational systems within which social identities can be established and transmitted through enculturation . . . creating a culturally grounded social identity that included the expectation of cooperation among kin" (2020:194).

An animal that is naturally individualist, competing with other animals, cannot create a society capable of enforcing rules. One cannot make mountain lions form social contracts or teach crocodiles to cooperate. Hobbes,

Freud, and others expected far too much of human rationality. Rationality is notoriously unable to restrain emotion. A serious cost of the Hobbesian view, however, is assuming people are worse than they really are and excusing tendencies to act worse than expected. This Hobbesian view has always been popular with hatemongers.

The other classical and mistaken view of humanity is the rational self-interest view. The briefest look at humanity instantly dispels that. People do not act in their self-interest, and rarely act rationally in that restricted sense (Kahneman 2011). The "irrational" heuristics that people use can be highly useful as shortcuts, creating mental efficiency (Gigerenzer 2007; Gigerenzer et al. 1999), but they constantly cause trouble when cool reason is needed. Human limits to rationality are well documented. Certainly, genocide has little rational excuse.

However, the rationalist view is a more positive view of humanity than Hobbes' or Freud's. It does not give much space to evil, explaining that evil occurs only in unusual cases when it really pays off in material terms. Unfortunately, irrational evil is common. Tyrants may sometimes die in bed, but they often do not. Suicide bombers, school shooters, and other front-line fighters for evil are obviously not advancing their rational self-interest. Shortsighted but "rational" calculation does explain some bad action, but does not explain people paying enormous personal costs to be hateful and cruel. It also fails to explain the common human tendency to resist improving themselves and their surroundings. Over the 5,000 years of recorded history, countless people around the world have chosen to suffer and make themselves miserable simply to hurt others or to maintain bad habits in the face of better advice. Technology has often been developed for war. Rational choice could be believed as a motive only because irrational hate, vengefulness, overreaction to slights, and the like are so common that they seem "rational" or may not even be noticed.

A more realistic, but still dubious, description on human natures comes from the Zoroastrian-Manichaean tradition. This tradition views people as a mixture of well-meaning, prosocial good and cruel, brutal evil. It further holds that good comes from the immaterial "spirit" realm and evil from the flesh. This view, which entered Christianity with St. Paul (Letter to the Romans), lies behind the extreme puritanism of much of Western society—the view of sex, good food, good wine, and dancing as naughty and sinful. Everything of the flesh tends toward corruption. Good sex is the door to hell. "The fiddle is the devil's riding horse," according to one American proverb. The authors of this book were raised in a time and place when such views were widespread. The social revolution of the 1960s eroded these views, but they keep resurfacing. H. L. Mencken in *A Mencken Chrestomathy* defines puritanism as "the haunting fear that someone, somewhere, may be happy" (1949:624). Yet, a great deal of human good comes via those "sins." Condemning these is regularly used to distract people from the real sins: cruelty, oppression, gratuitous harm, selfish greed, and hatred.

A deeper problem with the Manichaean view is that people are usually neither saintly nor demonic. They are just trying to make a living and then get some rest and relaxation. Their forays into proactive goodness or proactive evil are extensions from the ordinary low profile of getting along. The Native American folktale of the two wolves, like the "good and bad angels" of folk Christianity and before that from Manichaean belief, are symbols of the prosocial and hostile sides of human nature. In this sense, people are neither good nor bad; they are good to kin and to culturally constructed fictive kin, bad to rivals, and neutral to everyone else. There is a very slight positive bias, enough to have saved the human race so far, but people will kill vast numbers of distant strangers without thinking much about it, as King Leopold of Belgium did—indirectly—in the Congo.

In short, people are far better than the imaginary "savages" of Hobbesian and Freudian writings, but not as good as idealists or rationalists assume. The hopeful dreams of "positive psychology" and "humanistic psychology" have turned to dust. Ordinary everyday human life is full of minor slights, often incorrectly interpreted as personal attacks. It is also full of minor kindnesses. We are always poised near the edge of flipping into violence or heroism. From this constant low-level evil and good, it is easy to move suddenly and unexpectedly to much greater evil or good. Everyday good can be stimulated by situations or by moral persuasion, and people can be heroic. Often the contrast is between the cynical "realism" of evildoers and the "unrealistic" idealism of the best in human nature. People often must choose ideals or be lost to the cynics.

We are gifted by our mammalian heritage with the ability to love, care, fear, hate, and fight. These qualities we share with all higher mammals. We are also gifted with the uniquely human ability to form complex, diverse social and cultural systems that construct care, fear, aggression, and other natural drives in ways that can amplify both good and evil.

FIGHT, FLIGHT, FREEZE

The first stage in understanding violence is grounded in the whole complex of animal responses to threat. All mammals, or almost all, fight over resources (Clutton-Brock 2016). These can include food, space, holes for dens, and anything else that is necessary but limited. Usually, males fight over access to females. All social mammals fight for dominance in social hierarchies. To cope with this, all have a fight-flight-freeze response to threat, stress, and sudden loss. Higher animals—not just humans—have a grief response to serious loss. This grief can spark its own fight-flight-freeze response. Anger after a death is normal in humans, along with withdrawal, escape, and simply bearing it (Kubler-Ross 2014).

Most mammals know when to stop. Fights are rarely to the death. Fighting over females and over dominance within the pack usually end when one contestant is losing, and gives up with gestures of submission. Another well-known observation is that predators killing prey deploy a quite different set of behaviors (and neurological correlates) from the same predators fighting each other. Anyone with a cat knows this: the cat hunts for mice in a systematic, cool, quiet way, trying to stay unnoticed, but fights other cats in a highly dramatized way—raising fur and stretching up to look big, screaming and spitting, snarling, showing fangs, and generally being as conspicuous as possible. Quite different brain networks are entrained for these activities. Cats will toy with prey, cruelly by our standards, but they certainly do not make calm social decisions to starve millions of their fellows to death. Some social animals—ranging from chimpanzees to meerkats—eliminate competing groups in a coldly systematic fashion that disturbs many observers. Chimpanzees have provided a model of a violent, scary animal uncomfortably close to humans.

The fight-flight-freeze response is wired into the nervous systems (Sapolsky 2017, 2018). It is turned on by the bone-generated hormone osteocalcin (Columbia University Irving Medical Center 2019; ScienceBeta 2019) and then mediated by adrenaline. Faced with superior strength and an escape route, an animal will flee; with no escape, it will freeze if cornered and attacked; it will fight, even against superior strength. This response is mediated through the ancient limbic system in the lower back part of the brain. A threat is first processed by the amygdala, which recognizes and catalogues it (the amygdala being also a center of memory, as well as the center of much emotionality). A message goes to the hypothalamus, where the center of the fight-flight-freeze response occupies a small group of nuclei that mediate aggressive behavior, increased heart rate, elevated blood pressure, and directing blood toward appropriate muscle and nerve systems. This area sends messages down to the pituitary gland, attached to the bottom of the hypothalamus. Hormones are released from the anterior pituitary, and circulate through the body, stimulating—among other things—release of adrenaline and cortisol from the adrenal glands (Fields 2019).

All this is under varying degrees of control from the frontal and prefrontal cortex—very little in a lizard, a great deal in a well-socialized human. In a human, *the frontal cortex makes you do the harder thing when it's the right thing to do* (Sapolsky 2017:45, emphasis his). That can mean doing what is reasonable, foregoing a reward now for a bigger one later, or what is social, foregoing a theft because it is morally wrong. Stress, however, disorients. Sustained stress and fear lead to chronic biologic responses that impair judgment and lead to heightened responses (Sapolsky 2017). Under such conditions, animals and people can flip almost instantly from peaceful, calm behavior to extreme violence. This is the biological substrate of the sudden change from good wolf to bad wolf. Humans have complicated the response. We are faced, more than other animals, with a tradeoff between reacting emotionally and rationally. The medial frontal cortex, home of social emotionality, dominates empathetic and sensitive choices, and—with other regions—cognitive empathy (Kluger et al. 2019; Lombardi 2019). The dorsolateral prefrontal cortex is more involved with "cool, utilitarian choices" (Kluger et al. 2019:12). The ventromedial prefrontal cortex integrates many of these, and processes morality and its social applications, as well as cognitive interaction choices. It is conspicuously absent in the reaction of psychopaths to pain of others (Lombardi 2019). More interesting, in psychopaths, is their lack of connection between the reward processing center of the brain—the ventral striatum—and the center for examining outcomes and consequences, including emotional ones, in the ventral medial prefrontal cortex (Lombardi 2019). A quite different situation is found in people on the autism spectrum, who may be socially challenged but are generally well-meaning, trying hard but often failing to be social; damage to the anterior cingulate cortex is suspected. It seems that differences in brain regions and connections lie behind a great deal of human good and evil. This does not explain why the same individual or group can transition so rapidly from one to the other.

People have an innate tendency to become hateful, cruel, and violent. It is not a mere ability that society trains into us. The generalized cognitive abilities to make computers, drive cars, and trap fish in weirs can be performed by any trained human of reasonable intelligence, but humans do not have any innate tendencies for these specific tasks. They do not make computers unless taught, within a society with a long history of technological development. Evil is different. Every known cultural and social group in the history of the world has had its cruel, murderous individuals, and the horrible record of wars and genocides proves that almost every human will act with unspeakable cruelty under social pressure.

To return to the fight-flight-freeze response: First, one must identify a threat. Then one must decide whether to react with flight or fight and how much flight or fight to apply. This requires attention to what is actually causing the threat. If one is being chased by a bear, no questions need be asked, but dealing with widespread social problems is something quite different. Reasonable alternatives include freezing: distancing oneself, resenting silently, turning the other cheek, being as pleasant or fearless as possible, or just bearing hardship. From there, the next step is to actual caring and working together.

Thus, in humans and to some extent in other higher animals, fighting, fleeing, and freezing are supplemented by a fourth recourse: *rational coping*. The most basic cut is between courageous defense, which is only deployed at need and to the extent needed, and irrational panic, which is excessive and hurtful. Then one must plan how to deploy resources for maximum protection. Irrational violence and harm take over when rational coping fails and a fight response is triggered. Humans are special in another, and very disturbing, way: we carry grudges, plot for years, and become malignant. All intelligent and social animals do this to some extent—many of us have known dogs and horses who remember who abused them, and attack the abuser years later—but only humans can do it at a more than minor level. Animals may attack weaker pack members without warning following abuse by stronger, more dominant packmates; humans seem to have carried this forward, to scapegoat whole populations, something otherwise not found among other animals. Human reason, in the sense of ability to plan at high levels of abstraction, allows us to flourish and to help others, but in the service of anger it allows us to hate and oppress beyond the capacity of any other animal. In people, because of the necessity to prioritize dealing with threat, hate is all too often stronger than love, viciousness stronger than caring, defensive resistance to change stronger than desire for self-improvement. Overreaction to threat is selected for. Assuming a poisonous snake is a rope is far less adaptive than assuming a rope is a snake (to use the classic Indian example). Failure to find food in a given day means a better hunt tomorrow, but failure to identify a deadly threat means no tomorrow. Even plants react with fear; they deploy defenses when attacked by predators (Walters 2017).

This is the ultimate biological substrate of human reactions, including the human tendency to overreact to perceived or imagined threat. Humans seem about half dedicated to crushing opposition, from criticism to competition, and half dedicated to peacefully obtaining what they need and wish. Feedback in perceived threat—deadly spirals—is made probable by the need to react to even mild threat as potentially serious. Contingent variation in personal, situational, and cultural factors prevents better prediction than a rough 50–50 split.

John Tierney and Roy Baumeister, in *The Power of Bad* (2019), are the most recent authors to state this obvious fact. Chronic threat and stress crystallize the fight response into hatred, the flight response into escapism, and the freeze response into conformity or apathy. Tierney and Baumeister write of the widespread human tendency to react to the worst or most threatening fact: long friendships broken by a single word, engagements broken off because of a birthday forgotten, perfect holidays ruined by one accident.

More relevant to our concerns here is the tendency of humans to hate and fear a whole group because a few of its members act conspicuously badly. This is observed among both conservatives and liberals. Polls often mis-predict how people will act: people generally answer that they want positive benefits, such as more wages, or better health care, but then vote or act their hate rather than their self-interest. They may be lying, but often they really do mean their words, only to vote their hatred when emotions overwhelm them at the last minute. This leads to massive misprediction of election results, as happened in the United States in 2016.

Tierney and Baumeister also acknowledge the human tendency to be over-optimistic. This usually comes from confidence, trust, and good will—the good wolf, well fed—but it can come from fear, via the defense mechanism of denial. Abused spouses, especially women, commonly display this. One sees it on a larger scale in much of the "humanistic psychology" literature. It took massive denial to trust human potential so soon after World War II, but many in those days were confident that good had triumphed in that war and would continue to triumph until the world was renewed. It never occurred to those of us who went through the dreamy 1960s that the United States would drift toward fascism within our lifetimes. We were in denial.

Flight can thus be into video games and daydreams, freezing can be labeled "depression" or "laziness" by psychologists or judgmental peers, and human fighting is usually verbal rather than violent. Still, all the limbic responses are there, underlying the prefrontal plans and cultural instructions that introduce the complexity. (For this and for what follows, see Bandura 1982; Baumeister 1997; Beck 1999; Caprara 2002; Ellis 1962; Maslow 1970; Staub 2011.)

The most basic root of aggression is fear (LeDoux 2015). Any animal capable of fighting will fight when threatened or attacked, if there is no alternative. This involves fear of loss of necessary resources, but often—especially with mates—it is simply fighting to win desired goods. Sheer discomfort—sickness, hunger, loss—can also make most animals more aggressive or fight-prone. The order follows: stressors; feeling of inadequacy or frustration; defensiveness; then, if the bad wolf wins, hatred and aggression. Grief can also be a source of stress and thus of violence. The role of grieving in motivating suicide bombing has been addressed by Atran (2010). In many cultures, from Appalachia to New Guinea, grief over previous killings leads to expected revenge. Chronic fear becomes anxiety, chronicled by Joseph LeDoux in his book *Anxious* (2015). Most humans spend a great deal of their time in a state of worry, anxiety, and negative feelings about the minor stresses and strains of life. Brooding about these problems is the most basic food of the bad wolf. Downstream effects of hatred and aggression include widespread fear, leading to disempowerment, discouragement (literally "discourage"), conformity, irresponsibility, and general lack of self-efficacy.

The human difference from other animals is that humans are compulsively and complexly social (Henrich 2016; Sapolsky 2017). They live for their social systems: families, communities, neighborhoods, networks, and—in the modern world—nations. Humans feel fear when these communities are threatened. Even humans not at all involved in a community will often feel fear or anger over seeing it attacked. People are willing to die for their communities. We routinely observe the heroism of soldiers sacrificing themselves in war, parents dying to save children, suicide bombers blowing up supposed enemies (Atran 2010; Bélanger et al. 2014), and even gang members dying for their drug gangs.

The usual human condition, socially constructed on the innate bases described above, seems to be kind, friendly, and warm to one's in-group, hospitable to strangers, hostile to opponent groups in one's own society, and deeply hostile to individuals in one's own society who seem to be a threat to one's control or standing, or to society's most fundamental beliefs. Threats to social beliefs lead to savage persecution of "heretics." Heretics and minority religions are the victims of many of the very worst massacres. They usually live mixed in among the orthodox. Perhaps the intimacy is related to the extreme violence of such persecutions. Cognitive dissonance can make people act worse than they might.

It is also universally known that people are most easily united by being confronted with a common threat, especially a human threat—an invading army, looting gangs, or simply those "heretics." Leaders tend to seek or invent enemies. Existential threat—fear of death—exacerbates hatred. In a fascinating study, Park and Pyszczynski (2019) found that making fear of death salient to experimental subjects made them become more defensive about their group identification and core values, and more intolerant and antagonistic toward others. They found, moreover, that mindful meditation could reduce this, and eliminate it in practiced meditators, unleashing an unexpected, potentially important weapon against hate.

THE EVOLUTION OF VIOLENCE

Any animal must divide its attention between avoiding threat and getting necessities of life. Real wolves—as opposed to the ones inside us—have their own fights; normally peaceful and calm, they erupt into violence when a new wolf threatens an established pack, or when a bear or human enemy attacks (Clutton-Brock 2016). Dogs, domesticated descendants of wolves, still engage in "resource guarding"; an otherwise peaceful dog, especially if leashed, may attack anyone that seems to menace its owner. Humans, with far more complex social lives than other animals, add socially constructed identifications with groups, their basic principles, and their identifying markers, which can range from skin color to religious beliefs.

Excessive need for control is notably a part of the profile of violence. In many species of mammals, including humans, males will kill other males and even their own female companions to maintain control of females (Clutton-Brock 2016; Heid 2019). Intraspecific aggression and violence are universal in higher animals, highly structured, and shaped by evolution (Clutton-Brock 2016). Even meerkats, regarded by many humans as particularly cute, are murderous to rival groups; females will hunt out and kill pups of neighboring packs (Clutton-Brock 2016:303). The rapid transition from harmony, empathy, playfulness, and cooperation to cold-blooded murder of weaker "others" is not confined to humans, or even to large predators like wolves.

We evolved from animals that presumably fought for mates and territory, leading to some propensity for genocide and mass violence in human evolution. Tratner and McDonald (2020) argue that males are simply evolved to kill. They proceed to undermine their case by discussing the roles of ideology, politics, and the like in structuring mass murder. If human males were killer apes, one would see small-scale violence frequently, as among chimps, but *not* the alternation between total peace and insane mutual destruction as evidenced in Rwanda and Cambodia, let alone the change in Scandinavia from Vikings to model peacekeepers.

That alternation requires the exact opposite of instinct. It requires people exquisitely attuned to culture and social situation. Even bridging from instinctive violence to ordinary barroom brawling, domestic abuse, to cultural violence and finally to genocide does not work. Abuse and brawling are culturally structured, with huge differences in incidence among and within cultural groups. Mass killing in this continuum is even less well correlated. Both peaceable, nonviolent cultural groups and chronically violent ones have been among the ranks of genociders.

An innate capacity for violence must underlie genocide and war, and young males tend to be more violent than other demographics in almost all mammal species, but this observation is only the beginning of an explanation of human violence. One social and cultural force is pressure on young men to prove themselves by acts of social daring or self-sacrifice. In warlike or violent societies, and sometimes even in peaceful ones, young men are under extreme pressure to be soldiers, fighters, or just "bad dudes." Young men are high in aggression and testosterone, but they are peaceful enough in peaceful societies. Their energies are used in work, sports, community service, or studying. But in warrior societies it becomes "toxic masculinity."

THE EVOLUTION OF COOPERATION

Humans are innately "moral," in the sense that they have natural predisposi-tions to fairness, generosity, tolerance, welcoming, acceptance, sociability, friendliness, and other social goods (Bowles and Gintis 2011; de Waal 1996; Henrich 2016; Reynolds 2020; Tomasello 2016, 2019). It is basically a rediscovery of what Mencius knew in the fourth century BCE. Anger at real harms, desire to satisfy basic wants, and desire for pleasure and beauty are universal human traits. Less pleasant universal traits include hatred of non-conformists, tendency to seize resources from others, and resentment for real or imagined slights.

Particularly relevant to our case are two very distinctive things about humans. First, we can form higher-order, recursive plans: deploy tactics because of strategies directed at objectives that will accomplish our goals, and combining sounds into words that make sentences that build into whole texts that communicate those plans in detail. Second, we can cooperate to an almost unlimited extent in carrying out our plans, whether for good or for ill.

Michael Tomasello and Richard Wrangham have studied the duality of human nature in producing both violence and cooperation. Michael Tomasello, in *A Natural History of Human Morality* (2016), postulates that morals evolved in three steps. First came natural sympathy, developed from the loving emotions that all higher mammals feel for their mothers and sib-lings. These are extended to other kin and ultimately to any close associate in human society. Infants display this ability from birth. Second, as humans evolved cooperative hunting and foraging, they learned to share with and support their partners. Apes do not do this; they may cohunt but they do not share or cooperate more than minimally. However, wolves and meerkats do. Third, and uniquely human, all social groups have cultural moral repertoires. They have long lists of "oughts," almost always said to be supernaturally sanctioned.

Tomasello follows other evolutionary thinkers in arguing that this human tendency to cooperate evolved in foraging. Cooperative animals could hunt big game, find isolated honey trees, and work together to catch fish. He misses the parallel with wolves. Canids scaled up from foxlike mouse hunt-ers to large pack animals who could hunt big game. However, their need to run fast denied them the chance to develop the formidable claws that allow cats to be solitary hunters of big animals. Wolves must cooperate to chase and bring down large animals. This skill is seen today in the incredible skills of herding dogs at coordinating their efforts. They not only have to know exactly what each other dog is thinking and planning, but they must also put themselves in the positions of the humans and the sheep. We once watched with awe as two shepherds and their sheepdogs negotiated a herd of sheep through a difficult traffic intersection in the Pyrenees. The shepherds did almost nothing; the dogs worked together, trusting each other to keep order in a dangerous environment, while understanding both what the shepherds wanted and what the sheep would do. They managed this three-species balancing act perfectly, demonstrating a "theory of mind" that included a stunning ability to coordinate, integrate, and cooperate across species. Recently in the jungles of central India, BA witnessed another kind of superb cross-species cooperation. The huge sambar deer is generally the first animal to emit a warning bark about the approach of a foraging Bengal tiger. Then there is a chain reaction with other species, rhesus monkeys, high in the trees, contributing noisy GPS-type mapping. In response is rapid, kinesthetic action from ground-dwelling creatures making the location message quite salient. In short, cooperation in ordinary life, in hunting, and in managing threats is not confined to humans, but humans have extended it far beyond anything other animals do (Boyer 2018).

Immanuel Kant's "deontological" ethics (Kant 2002) deduce rules from basic principles. Tomasello, a good Kantian, examines the rules underlying the basic principles of cooperation and mutualism, often citing the work of fellow Kantian Christine Korsgaard (1996) for this approach. In contrast, utilitarian "assertoric" ethics hold that ethics are practical solutions to everyday problems (Brandt 1979). It is clear, ethnologically, that both these methods of creating moral rules are common in everyday life and that every culture has a mix of high abstractions and pragmatic rules of thumb. Moral philosophers tend to emphasize one or the other, but cultural traditions balance both. Humans have culturally constructed moral rules that regulate large groups, involving millions of people who never meet at all. As Tomasello points out, children raised in human families learn these rules very early, but family pets do not (2016, 2019). Pets do learn to act differently in different cultures, but only through specific training. Tomasello (2016) admits that people are frequently immoral, but does not go into that side of life. He does not take into account the actual alternatives within cultural systems that allow people to murder each other for purely moral reasons, from Aztec human sacrifice to capital punishment. In a later publication (Tomasello 2019) he admits this conflict has something to do with shaping human moralities. Tomasello's optimistic view precludes him from addressing hatred, but one can assume, from his work, that nonhuman animals cannot really hate; it takes too much abstract thinking.

Tomasello sharply contrasts apes and human infants. Even before they can talk, human infants show a vibrant sociability more complex than chimpanzees. By the time they are three, children have reached not only a level of social sensitivity that outdoes the ape, but they also can think morally, reason according to what they see others doing and thinking, and react on the basis of anticipating what others expect. Apes barely do anything like this. They do show awareness of others' thoughts and fear of punishment and domination, but they do not understand abstract social rules. By the age of six, human children are rational, reasonable beings who know how to apply the moral and pragmatic rules of their cultures (Tomasello 2019); apes are left far behind.

Those of us who have introduced and raised children in multicultural settings are aware that children know by the time they are three years old that there are varying sets of social rules. By age six, children are masterful at language-shifting, rule-shifting, and norm-shifting depending on what group they are with. It was almost spooky to watch our young children, in various venues around the world. For instance, they quickly learned that a mass of undifferentiated words must be separated into "Chinese" (tonal, rhythmic, spoken with those outside the family) and "English" (a very different-sounding language used within the family). They matched culturally appropriate politeness behavior to the language.

Tomasello (2019) views humans as basically cooperative, helpful, generous, and moral (according to their societies' codes). Human children show astonishing levels of fairness by three years of age, in contrast to apes, who simply grab anything they want from weaker apes. However, much of his sample derives from childcare centers in rather genteel college towns. There are less harmonious child environments that force children to choose quickly between the two wolves. Richard Wrangham addressed this issue in his book *The Goodness Paradox* (2019). He contrasts reactive aggression—ordinary anger and rage leading to violence—with proactive aggression, which evidently started out as hunting (recall the cats mentioned above), but was retooled in human evolution as planned, cool-headed violence. Compared to other primates, humans have less reactive violence. Humans are far less violent than chimpanzees, being more like peaceable bonobos. On the other hand, humans display more proactive violence—our raids, organized crimes, wars, and genocides are premeditated, often cold-blooded rather than passionate.

Wrangham questions how we could have evolved with this duality of violence and cooperation. Some widespread human behavioral repertoires involve peaceful cooperation, such as foraging and food preparation, while others are proactively violent. He proposes that both arise from our ability to cooperate, especially to subdue excessively violent individuals. Even chimpanzees do this to some extent, and humans quite often do. Ethnographies recount stories of psychopathic or hyperaggressive persons being quietly eliminated. Four men will go out hunting, three will return, and no questions are asked. Wrangham follows Christopher Boehm (1999) in seeing this as elimination of violent forces disrupting harmony within traditional societies.

Wrangham further hypothesizes that proactive aggressive behavior happened frequently enough to influence human evolution, selecting against reactive aggression. Once cooperation was established and used in proactive aggression, it was available to allow one group to devastate a neighboring group (Wrangham 2019).

While this theory is consistent and plausible, there is no real evidence for it. No one has counted the number of persons eliminated by cooperative execution. Moreover, Wrangham weakens his argument by showing that cooperative execution is usually invoked against nonconformists, often meek and innocent ones, rather than against bullies and psychopaths. Bullies and psychopaths, themselves, often invoke the violence, executing weak competitors. This behavior would select for violence, rather than against it.

In any case, the point is made that there is a strong tendency for humans to form coalitions. Those who stand together prevail, wipe out less cooperative enemy groups, and leave more descendants. This is known as "parochial altruism" (Bowles 2006, 2008, 2009; Boyer 2018; Choi and Bowles 2007). Large-scale cooperative raiding and defense were common among hunter-gatherers, often with sacrifice of their own members (Keeley 1996; Turney-High 1949). Serious wars prevailed in large nonagricultural groups, for example, Northwest Coast, Plains, and California Native peoples. Wrangham (2019) finds little evidence of individual sacrificing life or security for the group in hunter-gatherer warfare. Individuals do not have to go out of their way to sacrifice themselves as long as they were adhering to group norms. A key point is that Wrangham's work focuses on tiny hunter-gatherer bands that do not have the manpower to support large coalitions and the resulting costs of lives lost.

A different view of the evolution of cooperation is provided by Samantha Lang and Blaine Flowers (2019). They begin from the other extreme: the phenomenon of individuals caring for others who have terminal dementia and thus can never pay back any debts (material or psychological) to their caregivers. The vast majority of such caregiving is within the family—60.5 percent from children, 18 percent from spouses, most of the rest from other relatives—but even this is "irrational" in economic terms, and even in biological terms, since it distracts the caregivers from investing more in their children. The residual 5 percent of care is often given by devoted volunteers, who simply want to help others. They note that all this can simply be seen as an "exaptation" from inclusive fitness—if we are selected to care for kin, we have to care for all kin. Other animals do not do this, although there are some anecdotal records of group-living predators supporting disabled members.

Oliver Curry, Daniel Mullins, and Harvey Whitehouse (2019) hold that people evolved through cooperation, and that cooperation was then constructed as morality. In their "morality-as-cooperation" theory, there are six basic values:

- "Allocation of resources to kin" (family values),
- "Coordination to mutual advantage" (group loyalty),
- "Social exchange" (reciprocity),
- "Contests between hawks and doves" (bravery and respect),
- "Division" (fairness),
- "Possession" (property rights) (Curry et al. 2019:54).

These are further subdivided in specific, widely held values, for example, family values start with "being a loving mother, being a protective father, helping a brother, caring for a frail relative" (Curry et al. 2019:54). They examined sixty societies around the world, reporting that among well-studied societies all have these values, except for limited data on division (fairness).

COOPERATION AS AN EVOLVING HUMAN TRAIT

Selection originally operated, as in all higher animals, through inclusive fitness: mutual care is deployed among families to maximize genetic success over time. This then can be extended along ever-wider kinship lines, and to increase in scope to include in-marrying spouses. This has generally been the bride in most traditional human societies, although in many agricultural societies, it is the groom who moves. The need to marry out is not only to prevent inbreeding but also to build solidarity with neighbor groups. This means that selection cannot totally favor one's own genetic investment all the time. There is a paradox: one can maximize one's own genetic advantage only by having children with a genetically different mate. The classic arguments for genetic determination of selfishness all founder on this rock.

The scope increases when kinship includes whole communities, including in-laws, distant cousins, adopted children, and fictive or culturally constructed relatives such as blood brothers and "courtesy aunts." By this time, the link with genetics is essentially lost. Huge groups characterize modern society in which we freely adopt strangers' children, marry people from other countries, and devote our lives to helping humanity. However, a well-known social fact is that we continue to privilege close family members and to build solidarity with others by self-consciously using family terms: band of brothers, sisterhood, godchild, godmother, church father.

A widely known proverb summarizes this strategy for solidarity: "I against my brother; my brother and I against our cousin; my cousin, brother, and I against our village; and our village against the world!" (See Voorhees et al.

2020; they give a slightly different version.) The more closely related we are to others, the more solidarity we feel with them. Aggregating along kinship lines allowed Genghis Khan and his followers to build world-conquering armies. They widely extended kinship claims while tolerating huge differences. On the other hand, the closer we are to others, the more we are psychologically involved with them, the more we care about their opinions, depend upon their help, and experience hurt and anger in interactions with them.

Solidarity in the face of attack by an enemy group is an evolved norm. Since larger groups tend to kill off smaller groups, overlapping cores of relatives through widened kin selection provides solidarity. Samuel Bowles (2006, 2008) discussed the tendency of kinship groups to demand solidarity and loyalty as well as detect and punish disloyal members. Violence against outgroups evolved along with this detection and punishment of nonreciprocity within groups. In defense against an attacking enemy, group loyalty demands conformity and confrontation.

Most small-scale societies, according to ethnographic records, are or were peaceful internally but often at war with neighbors. Moreover, they can rapidly change the definitions of "us" and "them," to create coalitions, to form alliances with former enemies, and to attack former friends. These facts are impossible to explain from older models of human behavior. How could Hobbesian "savages" or Freudian "ids" differentiate so cleanly? How could virtuous "noble savages" be so bloody to their neighbors? How could people change affiliations so easily? One view is that ordinary persons can be strongly motivated, usually by leaders, to support their group if there is perceived conflict with another group. Another consideration is posttraumatic stress disorder (PTSD), an area well-researched by the National Institute of Mental Health. Humans, like other mammals, are profoundly altered by extreme and ongoing stress, especially abuse by or conflict with other people. However dysfunctional, PTSD is a self-protective, withdrawal response to a situation that destroys innate peacefulness or at least an innate reaction against violence. Strong social support is protective against PTSD. (See https://www.nimh.nih.gov/health/topics/post-traumatic-stress-disorder-ptsd/index.shtml.)

Groups compete for all kinds of scarce resources. In the presence of adequate food, larger groups will outcompete smaller ones, and will have enough genetic diversity within themselves to allow endogamy. The ideal group size seems to be around 50–150, which, in fact, is the size of the usual human face-to-face group (Dunbar 2010). Such groups tend to be parts of larger associations, typically around 500, a figure consistent from the number of speakers of a given language in hunting-gathering societies to the number of Facebook friends that a moderately sociable person has. Frequently, in small-scale societies, groups of fifty are exogamous, but groups of 500 are largely endogamous (Dunbar 2010).

In modern societies, groups cross-cut each other, and an individual may have one reference group that is "neighbors," another for "workmates," another for "religious congregation," and another for "hobby." Small-scale societies have little of this (Boyer 2018). Groups and loyalties shift, a point highly relevant to understanding cooperating and to framing genocide, where individuals suddenly change from thinking of "neighbor" to "ethnic foe" with subsequent discrimination and even murder. In the case of genocide, individuals shift their thinking back to the original "neighbor" category after the genocide. Hollie Nyseth Brehm's studies of Rwanda (Nyseth Brehm 2017a, 2017b) notably attest this phenomenon. It is one of the most significant aspects of genocide.

Recently, Mauricio González-Forero and Andy Gardner (2018) tested various models of cooperation consistent with the incredibly fast evolution of the human brain, which more than tripled in size in 2 million years. These authors took into account the origin and dispersal of humans from East Africa between 150,000 and 70,000 years ago. Their enterprise was highly speculative, but at least they had considerable data on the genetics, dispersal rates, and behavior of the humans in question. They concluded that models of human evolution that support conflict and violence are not consistent with rapid brain development. The cost of conflict is too high. Cooperation is necessary for survival. Voohees et al. support this this premise, "Although humans may act in spectacularly uncooperative ways and nonhuman animals sometimes appear to act cooperatively . . . human cooperation is unique in its degree and scope" (2020:194). Animals that fight all the time cannot develop large brains and in fact, often do not survive at all. Witness the mortality rate of the Tasmanian devil. However, if cooperation is limited, exclusive coalitions and Harff's "exclusionary ideologies" may hurt solidarity or even survival (Aalerding et al. 2018; De Dreu et al. 2016). Human cooperation is all too well demonstrated in oppression and persecution.

Sociability is another factor in brain development. Simple sociability does not contribute to fast brain development. González-Forero and Gardner (2018) found that highly social animals generally have smaller brains than closely related, less social species. Caretaking and mutuality substitute for enhanced thinking capacity. A bigger brain is needed. They conclude that only ecology can account for human brain development. A bigger, better brain enables animals to find more and better food which in turn creates a positive feedback loop, enabling brain development that helps humans to seek out and crave nutritious food, share information on food sources, and cooperate within a large kinship group. Graeber and Wengrow (2018) hold that humans probably evolved in larger and more complex groups than usually thought, and while conflict occurred, it was more efficacious to cooperate. E. N. Anderson (2014) points out that any animal that can find rich patches of food and communicate this information within a large kinship group has a huge advantage over competitors.

González-Forero and Gardner have not explained how cooperation breaks down and humans became so violent. Wrangham (2019) proposes that larger groups employed predatory expansion and resource grabbing against smaller, less powerful groups outweighs the benefits of cooperation. Predatory expansion historically has resulted in killing off the food supply. Most human groups have learned how to manage sustainably, but they often overshoot, and in many cases the learning was done the hard way. Myths and folktales recount stories of overhunting and then starving. As children, we both were subjected to cautionary tales about the social impact of greed, selfishness, sharing, and fair allocation of resources. We have passed on these same stories to our children.

SUMMARY

This chapter has explored theories of human nature, common responses of all animals to innate threats, the evolution of both violence and cooperation, and evolving traits in cooperation among humans. Chapter 5 focuses on norms and responses to violent and cooperative behaviors within the tapestry of individual and cultural variations.

Chapter 5

Individual and Cultural Variation

INDIVIDUAL VARIATION

Many factors make some individuals more violence-prone than others. All humans must satisfy basic physiological needs, including physical needs not only for food, water, and health, but also for security, control of life, and sociability. Also, they vary along these dimensions of personality—extraversion, openness, conscientiousness, agreeableness, and emotionality, according to the "Big Five" (see Soto and John 2017) and "Hexaco" personality theories; Hexaco adds an additional sixth dimension, honesty-humility. These dimensions, however, do not directly predict levels of violence, aggression, competitiveness, dominance, or hatred. Social pressures are also determinants. For instance, some people who are very low in openness may become conservatives and some evolve into in fascism; those who are very high in openness may become liberals and even evolve into fanatic rebels. However, most persons at both ends of openness exhibit decent behaviors most of the time.

Individual Ways of Difference

Personality traits are partially heritable. Some are influenced by early environmental conditions, modifying the genome through epigenetics. All are modified by learning, such as how to express anger, how to be violent, and whom to hate. Social and cultural learning is directly involved in expression of violence in all cultures. The agreeableness continuum is especially relevant to dominance, violence, and subsequent genocide. In this scale, there is dichotomy between agreeableness versus hostility, tolerance versus hatred, peacefulness versus violent aggression, help versus gratuitous harm, reasonableness versus unreason, open-minded versus closed, and charity versus greed. Those high on antagonism and aggression are susceptible to inflammatory rhetoric and heavily overrepresented among doers of evil (Kaufman 2018). These variants shape their responses to the good wolf and the bad wolf.

Low serotonin levels and low monoamine oxidase A levels are somewhat correlated with aggression (Alvarez and Bachman 2017). Gut microbiota is proposed to affect violent behavior. At least we know that certain microbiota can make aggressive mice more sociable (Sherwin et al. 2019). Antisocial personality disorder, including psychopathy and sociopathy, is a major "risk factor," but not "cause," of violent behavior (Alvarez and Bachman 2017:46–48). Although debated, the frustration-aggression hypothesis is one explanation—anger turning to resentment and sometimes to violence (Alvarez and Bachman 2017). Sociopaths or psychopaths are people who appear to have been born without a moral compass and any way of acquiring one. They seem incapable of acting without harming someone. Unlike most persons, including those with autism who lack social skills in perception, psychopaths and hyperaggressive persons seem to have preternatural social skills. "Psychopaths . . . understand what others are feeling but have a profound lack of empathetic concern" (Denworth 2017:61; cf. Baskin-Sommers et al. 2016). They may have anomalies in neural connections in the brain that affect agreeableness.

Serial killers are more deficit in the agreeableness trait than ordinary psychopaths. The one mass murderer ENA has known was severely disturbed. By contrast, people we both have known who have killed others, including soldiers, threatened refugees, women in life-threatening domestic violence situations, are, to one extent or another, quite traumatized by the experience.

Sociopaths and psychopaths, low in empathy, are residents of a different world. They lie without a second thought, and, even when it clearly is against their better judgment, they seem to prefer dealing treacherously and unfairly with others. Ordinary rational self-interest simply does not work for them. We have known several who wrecked their lives by wholly gratuitous betrayal. They simply could not understand why betraying others brought outrage. Some psychopaths and sociopaths can be successful in business, politics, and leading genocides, partly because of their supreme self-confidence and indifference to criticism. They are often suave, politically sophisticated, and lacking a sense of guilt. Based upon crime rates, calculation of voting patterns for extreme candidates, and surveys of the prevalence of psychopathy and violent ideation, about 10 percent of the population may have some of these characteristics.

Individuals who turn violent may also show social dominance orientation (Altemeyer 2010; Guimond et al. 2013), looking favorably upon economic inequality and inequitable social organization. While most mammals have dominance hierarchies, Boehm (1999) claims that humans lack innate tendencies in that direction (others disagree; see Boyer 2018). Even so, oppressive hierarchic systems develop, often led by tyrants of low agreeableness and high dominance. Frank Chuang and collaborators report, "Hierarchy privileges conformity, order and security" (Chuang et al. 2020:4034). Strongly hierarchic societies encourage scorn and even hatred of those below, and of those conspicuously "different" in important ideological ways. In a hierarchy, one must constantly worry about maintaining one's position and preventing rivals and those below from taking over.

The author Kurt Vonnegut created a character who survived the Nazi Holocaust: "She was asked what she had learned from the Holocaust, and she said she learned that 10 percent of any population is cruel, no matter what, and that 10% is merciful, no matter what, and the remaining 80 percent could be moved in either direction" (from Kurt Vonnegut Museum and Library posting, https://www.facebook.com/VonnegutLibrary/posts/1015423461565 0209, retrieved March 30, 2020). There is a continuum of individuals who are the most evil to ordinary middling souls to saints. Those 10 percent of low agreeableness-highly dominant individuals can be socially balanced by those who are highly agreeable. The best 10 percent are unfailingly kind and sensitive, give donations freely, and devote their lives and careers in healing, teaching, and helping. The other 80 percent are those, like most of us, deal constantly with the two wolves. We struggle from acceptance to rejection, positive to negative-sum gaming, laudable ambition to power-madness, necessary defense to defense based on cowardly fear. We drive too fast. We eat junk food. We take advantage of cheap deals when we know that workers are underpaid. We give nibbles to the bad wolf while trying to serve the good one. We dodge responsibilities and commit the "deadly sin" of sloth. In short, we are frail and fallible humans, needing strong social and ethical standards backed up by law to keep us on the straight and narrow path (Henrich 2016).

This collective continuum of differences among individuals spans the demented psychopath, the ordinary criminal, the schoolyard bully who evolves into a spouse abuser, the grumbler, the person who struggles with temper, the person who is a model of strength within the family, community, or nation. People everywhere range from very bad to very good, passive to active, weak to strong—the classic three dimensions of agentive evaluation (Osgood et al. 1957). Thus, humanity witnesses this impact of individuality imposed upon endless cycles of tranquility and violence.

Society ideally exists to preserve the good and to redirect the bad to fighting "the enemy" rather than each other. Loyalty to a functioning workgroup or community is necessary to normal human life; we work together, support each other, and look out for each other. It never works perfectly. If the worst 10 percent are dominant enough, many of the 80 percent, apathetic or enmeshed in frustration and hate, will be convinced to vote their hate against their self-interest. Hitler was elected with a bare plurality, not a majority, and the same is true of many elected evil leaders. Donald Trump was elected by 25.7 percent of the voting public. Almost half of registered voters did not bother to vote at all.

If most of the 80 percent and some of the best 10 percent can be corrupted and persuaded, the pendulum swings toward social hatred, control of people and resources, violence, and sometimes genocide. Petrarch (as quoted by Sarah Kyle 2017:157) stated, "The people strive to imitate all the actions and mannerisms of their prince. It is thus very true that no one harms the state more than those who harm by example. . . . The bad habits of rulers are harmful not only to themselves but to everyone." Extreme, high-emotion evil, grounded in hatred, ramped up, and modeled by some of the worst 10 percent, results in displaced aggression toward weaker people or a defenseless natural environment. The secret of the extremist aggressive individual is to make the deadliest links the most salient.

A genocidal individual will lead by appealing to a threatened or downwardly mobile majority. Recruiters for violent Islamic extremism, for instance, stress identification with Wahhabist Islam among those people who might otherwise see themselves as French, Moroccan, factory workers, soccer players, Malikite Muslims (the Malikite school values peace and tranquility), or other crosscutting loyalties. American fascists encourage susceptible recruits to view themselves primarily as those with "white privilege" or "heterosexual orientation" rather than as American citizens, farm workers, Christians, sports fans, or other loyalties that might provide competing ideologies to fascism. Once persuaded, whole populations will kill in perceived competition for goods, power, social standing, revenge, and "honor" (Alvarez and Bachman 2017; Anderson and Anderson 2013, 2017; Traverso 2019).

Individual Characteristics Promoting Violence

Unstable Self-Esteem

The most relevant individual characteristics that promote violence are weakness, insecurity, and tendency to anger—a recipe for defensiveness. These are people who are low in agreeableness, "have a chip on their shoulder," or "an attitude." Being simply weak and insecure makes one highly reactive to threat, but apt to be passive-aggressive about it. Being weak, insecure, *and angry*, whether dispositional or situational, leads to overreaction, escalation of defensive behavior, and often to violence. Being daunted and insecure, but physically strong and convinced of one's own fighting ability, leads to the barroom brawler and similar folk characters (Baumeister 1997). Tyrants are often living proof that a weak, insecure, angry person who assumes total power will still be a weak, insecure, and angry person.

When people are self-confident, secure, and self-controlled, whether dispositional or situational, they can damp down responses to challenge, and react rationally and coolly. Infants start without this self-efficacy (Bandura 1982), learning self-control as they develop. The strongest desire of humans is social belonging. People feel a strong need to conform to social norms. Acting reasonably good in concert with social norms seems the default option for most people most of the time. As pointed out by Kipling Williams (2007, 2011), few things are worse to people than ostracism after violating prevailing social norms. It was the worst punishment in ancient Greece. Baumeister documents the unexceptional nature of people who do evil things that are considered socially normative. They self-justify that they are doing the right thing and rationalize guilt, saying they are only doing what everyone does (1997). In genocides and slave camps, they are right; almost everyone in their situation is indeed doing it. It is, however, difficult to make people into killers. Not only the Nazis, but also armed forces everywhere, have always had trouble accomplishing this (Baumeister 1997).

People with unstable self-esteem are different. Baumeister, in his book *Evil*, demolishes the idea that evil people are those with low self-esteem; he proposes that the issue is their "high but *unstable* self-esteem" (1997:149; his emphasis). They are often bullies, thinking highly of themselves but insecure and easily wounded by challenges. They bolster their self-esteem by minimizing others. Basic predisposing factors of personality (threatened egotism, sadism, psychopathy) and immediate triggering factors (anger, greed, even idealism) feed into this behavior. All coveted goods, for example, material wealth, social position, or social acceptance, are won at the expense of other people, harming them in the process. These triggers do not cause this response in people who have high stable esteem. They are not in a chronic state of anger and hatred. Those who have fed the good wolf are satisfied by working with others for the common good and being accepted in society.

Bullying

Another key individual characteristic that promotes violence is bullying behavior. If people learn rational, esteem-building ways of coping with threat, fear, and anger, they are less likely to fall into hatred, bullying behavior, learned helplessness, and toxic conformity. If they fall into toxic conformity, they may become authoritarians. The "authoritarian personality" created by Freudian mechanisms (Fromm 1941) has not stood the test of time, but "authoritarian predispositions" leading to an "authoritarian dynamic" are now well attested and studied (Duckitt 1994, 2001; Stenner 2005). This dynamic is exacerbated especially by fear of the breakdown of the social norms that give what the authoritarian mind considers necessary structure to society. These norms typically espouse keeping minorities and women "in their place," and creating a rigid top-down order, often through bully behavior. Learned help-lessness among those with this authoritarian personality often leads to this toxic conformity (Peterson et al. 1993).

Michal Bilewicz (2020), building on John Duckitt's work, clarified research on the authoritarian personality with social dominance orientation characterized by arrogance and oppression. The exemplar is the Nazi ideology of racial superiority, violence, military expansion, and butchery of the weak (disabled and mentally ill, homosexuals, Roma and Jews) was a social construction from this social dominance base. People needed more than mere hate—they needed a whole complex of "ideals" to accompany it in order to hate downward. The Nazi philosophy implemented one of the most ideologically elaborated genocides in history. It employed a wide spectrum of ideologies and actors—underlings, saviors, heroic helpers (Bilewicz 2020).

Baron-Cohen (2011), Baumeister (1997), and Beck (1999) among others identified several subtypes of persons who despise or hate downward. The widest and most general category is those who simply believe in the neces-sity of hierarchies and of maintaining those hierarchies through keeping those below firmly in their place (Haidt 2012; MacIntyre 1984, 1988). An extreme form is the strongman philosophy that argues that rulers are above the law or are the law. Their most dedicated henchmen are weak, angry souls who desperately try to maintain their own position by maintaining the spiral of downward hatred.

Scared, defensive people easily fall victim to these bullying tactics used by strong authoritarian leaders. They parrot hatred and fear of homosexuals and other norm-benders, love of stringent punishment for lawbreakers (especially those low on the social scale), militarism, and rigid social divisions (Duckitt 1994, 2001). Their fear and weakness forbid aggressing against actual offend-ers; rather antagonism is displaced downward, scapegoating those less pow-erful (Copeland et al. 2014). Across the world, there is a range of ideology, from near-anarchist violence to more genteel responses, but the common denominator is a strong authoritarian leader who shows them how to mini-mize, blame, hate, and oppress underlings (Stenner 2005). The strong authori-tarian must be a bully with high unstable self-esteem, adulated as "strong" and "independent" by those who vicariously would love to have this power but are too weak. Instead, they become the followers, toadies, the "base."

Bullying involves belittling, minimizing, regarding others as worthless. The classic bully is resentful toward the world at large, attacking both the weak ("contemptible") and those in authority as well as reveling in breaking laws and conventions (Sapolsky 2017). Bullies resent civility; it interferes with their activities, and they brand it as "weakness." They resort to lying, insults, and "gaslighting" as methods of manipulating others. They tend to be violent and unpredictable, glorifying physical strength and devaluing intellectual qualities. A standard bullying routine is to insult the victim, then take any spirited response as an "insult" and "offense" that justifies attack. Imagined slights are quite adequate. The genociders' version of this is attribution of horrific but imaginary sins to a targeted group. Hitler's claims about the Jews are the most famous in this regard. Most movements that end in genocide, from ancient Greek demagogues to modern events, start by recruiting bullies and haters, whipping up escalating hatred, scapegoating less socially powerful groups, and often generating nativistic hate of foreigners, especially immigrants.

As Robert Sapolsky points out, "You want to see a kid who's really likely to be a mess as an adult? Find someone who both bullies *and* is bullied" (Sapolsky 2017:199; his italics). Serious bullies have almost always been abused physically (Alvarez and Bachman 2017; Batson 2011; Baumeister 1997; Zaki 2019). Being bullied can permanent negative effects on the brain of the growing child (Copeland et al. 2014).

Revenge

The third individual characteristic that promotes violence is revenge. Revenge is often the most terrible of motives. People tend to be at their very worst when revenging selves or others for slights, disrespect, or actual harms. This is a stimulus to torture and murder. All genociders eventually focus on a story theme that describes themselves or their community of identity as being victimized by the opponent. This opponent is frequently a group that is the least powerful but threatening to the status quo. Revenge is often for betrayal. It can create the vicious cycle so well portrayed in Shakespeare's play *Othello*—where, as so often in real life, the "betrayal" was a scam.

Social disrespect and slighting become pretexts for revenge, up to and including use of deadly force. Perceived physical weakness is a factor that may lead to antagonism toward the strong. Persons who are guiltily aware that they are prone to cut moral corners may attack "goody-goodies" (Parks and Stone 2010). Anti-intellectualism characterizes some people insecure about their own lack of self-improvement and education. They are rendered uncomfortable and experience learned helplessness either by direct insults or by seeing better-qualified but "inferior" people rise. Much of the anti-intellectualism and anti-"elitism" in the United States is propagated those in dominant groups who see people from less prestigious groups successfully moving up educational and cultural ladders. Conversely, the educated but insecure may turn from ordinary snobbery to worse offenses, as in Ezra Pound's embrace of fascism.

Forms of avenging violence reflect different personality profiles. Sheer aggressiveness, as a personality trait, is closely related to "oppositional personality disorder." Alienation, need for excessive control, excessive antagonism, resort to violence as first resort, or brooding or ruminating about real and imagined wrongs are some of the qualities among those who cope by avenging violence. Personality qualities may play some role, but a harsh, hostile, critical environment sprouts the seeds of discontent, the foods of the bad wolf. Baumeister describes "threatened egotism" (Baumeister 1997:377; Baumeister et al. 1996) as a catalyst to maintaining power and a deadly factor to precipitating revengeful behavior. Mass shooters, generally using high-powered assault rifles, are an example of the violent avenger. While rare, these shooters tend to be concentrated in war zones, or domestically in the United States. According to the studies, typically mass shooters are alienated young males, usually right wing. Most have been abused physically (Alvarez and Bachman 2017; Batson 2011; Baumeister 1997; Zaki 2019). In the United States, these shooters are often white supremacists targeting ethnic minorities (Cai et al. 2019). A recent study by Jillian Peterson and James Densley reported:

> The vast majority of mass shooters in our study experienced trauma and exposure to violence at a young age. Practically every mass shooter . . . reached an identifiable crisis point . . . leading up to the shooting . . . most of the shooters had studied the actions of other shooters. . . . Most mass public shooters are suicidal. (2019a:A11)

They further noted that the vast majority of the shooters in their study had revealed their plans to others but were not taken seriously, nor were their plans reported to authorities (Peterson and Densley 2019a).

In a subsequent report, these same authors related that mass murderers with a religious motivation have a similar profile. They examined eleven cases of mass shooters who targeted religious congregants. They described this population of avengers as follows:

- Male (n=11/11)
- History of substance abuse (n=9/11)
- Mentally in crisis at the time of the attack (n=9/11)
- History of mental illness (n=8/11)
- Suicidal (n=7/11)
- Most had recently been fired or changed jobs (Peterson and Densley 2019b:A9).

While the shootings were poorly planned, the shooters had with some known background in hatred, especially white supremacy or hatred of specified groups. However, several of the church shooters had smoldering anger at some or all of the religious congregants for personal reasons (Peterson and Densley 2019b:A9).

In context, it is worth noting that the majority of gun-related deaths domestically are either suicide or homicide of family or others in the immediate circle. They generally involve using cheap handguns (Alvarez and Bachman 2017).

In sum, high but *unstable* self-esteem, bullying, and motivations for revenge are life stresses. Among some very troubled individuals, coping with these stresses leads to violent or genocidal behavior. From these points, social pressures take over, defining groups to hate and sanctioning conformist behavior.

CULTURAL VARIATION

"Culture" is learned, shared knowledge and normative behavior within social groups, constructed over time by interaction among group members. While individual variation explains some aspects of violent behavior, culture provides a framework for violence. Culture includes shared knowledge about violence, conflict, dissent, anger, and conflict resolution (Beals and Siegal 1966). Canonical rules, models, and scripts are prescriptive, but cultural plans are flexible and can change (Beals and Siegal 1966). In a particularly violent period, such as World War II, or indeed in any sudden stressful situation (such as the Covid-19 pandemic), culture can change quickly as a society is forced to deal with new or threatening issues.

Scripts and Storylines

Culture provides models, scripts, and storylines, often symbolically embedded in literature. (See Homer's *Iliad*, Greek tragedies, Shakespeare's plays, China's *Three Kingdoms Story*, Japan's *Tale of the Heike*, Scottish ballads, and the latest Hollywood dramas of good and evil.) These, and Native American tales such as the story of the two wolves, often portray people in crisis forced to reveal their deepest selves and make choices between good and evil. Much of this literature turns on inescapable conflicts between two loyalties. These stories validate human agency; the protagonists are not mindless slaves of genetic endowment or of cultural shaping. An agent-based approach (in the tradition of Ibn Khaldun [1958] and Max Weber) demonstrates that humans do not just reflect their culture. These songs and stories turn on courage and cowardice, individuals against the world, opportunity, and failure. The hero or heroine is powerful against the storm, compelling both in form and predicament. Through drama, music, and dance, the cultural groups tell their stories.

Alternative storylines demonstrate that cultures are not homogeneous, and mindless conformity cannot work indefinitely. These stories are powerful in stripping away pretenses and revealing the roots of violence and human evil. While most cultural scripts are protective against violence, countervailing cultural instructions do not. For instance, Hitler drew upon centuries of well scripted plotlines glorifying pogroms and massacres against the Jews. Some contemporary Islamic teachings provide models for suicide bombing. Other cultural models glorify violence, speaking to "honor," berserker rage, battle frenzy, hatred, and bullying. Contemporary media portrayal is an example of cultural scripting. It has been shown to promote violent behavior among unstable, susceptible, and psychopathic people who identify with brutal heroes and villains (Alvarez and Bachman 2017). While brutality in ballads and theatrical drama is ancient, current media diffusion makes exposure ubiquitous. Fortunately, most people, most of the time, seem to be able to absorb media violence without turning violent themselves.

Cultural scripts define the use of weaponry in solving violent conflicts. While Swiss gun ownership is widespread, as all adult males are expected to be in readiness for national defense, gun killings are exceedingly rare in Switzerland. The United States, with about twice the gun ownership rate (Alvarez and Bachman 2017), has a much higher rate of gun-related homicide than Switzerland. American media often present gun homicide as heroic, or at least the best way to solve certain problems. Copycat shooting events in the United States are related to this cultural message rate (Alvarez and Bachman 2017).

Cultures of "Honor" and Escalation of Violence

Some cultures teach violent response to offenses as normative behavior (Baumeister 1997; Leung and Cohen 2011). Offense is easily taken, often leading to physical violence by men and verbal spitefulness among women (Nisbett and Cohen 1996). Defensiveness about social place and social position, that is, "honor" or "face," is a response to deep emotional wounding by social criticism and disrespect (Lefebvre 1992). The cultural instruction to such an offense is that one *should* overreact, escalating the conflict in order to preserve dignity. Extreme sensitivity to slights and willingness to die for trivial points of honor characterize such societies. If the violent reaction is not turned on the perpetrator, then the resentment is directed to scapegoats, usually culturally demeaned fractions of society. Bullying and abuse result. It involves a whole cognitive mindset, based on the assumption that life is unstable, and an individual, especially a male, must maintain honor and personal status at all costs and is dangerous if challenged (Lerro 2019; Nisbett and Cohen 1996). This pattern defines *cultures of honor* (Baumeister 1997; Henrich 2016; Nisbett and Cohen 1996). Brooding on slights and dishonors is the most inflammatory food for the bad wolf.

These honor cultures usually develop in places with high competition for resources but low governance in the sense of enforcement of law and order. These include border-warrior cultures at the fringes of old and oppressive civilizations, oppressed subcultures within dominant cultures, and subcultures of anomie and alienation. Descriptions and quoted statements of Caucasus fighters and American inner-city gangsters are astonishingly similar, and both are perfectly captured in the speeches of the characters in Shakespeare's medieval history plays.

Though the United States in general is not characterized by honor culture, the South in general and poorer segments of U.S. society do represent honor culture (Nisbett and Cohen 1996). The "Wild West" was wild for exactly this reason (see, for example, Mark Twain's account of gunslingers in *Roughing It*). Murders in the United States are concentrated among these subcultures that David Luckenbill has described the typical murder sequence in the United States as classical "murder-for-face" in a "character contest" (Alvarez and Bachman 2017:118–119). Individuals of low status everywhere may gravitate toward honor in this defensive sense (Henry 2009).

This creates a great deal of focus on loyalty and integrity in the "honor" code. The Mafia's savage *omertà* rules on retaliation against snitches provide a case in point. Shakespeare is brilliant in describing situations that provide maximal opportunities to betray your comrades, due to low level of governance and the level of aggressive group encounters. Consider the endless betrayals in Shakespeare's Henry VI and Richard III plays, with rapid shifts to whichever side looked stronger, accompanied by noble speeches. Shakespeare grew disillusioned with honor culture, or at least with its tendency to call forth hypocrisy. Iago, the most villainous villain in all literature, says to Othello: "Good name in man and woman, dear my lord, Is the immediate jewel of their souls: Who steals my purse steals trash; 'tis something, nothing; 'Twas mine, 'tis his, and has been slave to thousands; But he that filches from me my good name Robs me of that which not enriches him And makes me poor indeed" (Othello, Act III, Scene III). Later, Othello, realizing he murdered Desdemona because he was played for a fool by Iago, says: "An honourable murderer, if you will; For nought I did in hate, but all in honour" (Othello, Act V, Scene II).

Cultures of Religious Domination and Oppression

Religion usually includes peace, harmony, and nonviolence among its ideals, but it is also the source of foundational beliefs and foundational morals for most societies. It is an important source of security for many believers. Devout believers who depend on religion for both certainty and security often feel deeply and directly threatened by challenges to their faith. World religions eventually amass power via hierarchies and privileged initiations, furthering aggression in the context of violent defense. Social differences are often in the cultural construction of bullying, power-jockeying, and hatred which can become idealized and culturally taught via religion and other ideologies. Witness the inquisition, the crusades, and the Islamic wars of aggression.

True believers in any comprehensive ideology create gods who are either benign or a human-like mix of creative good with all-too-human foibles (like Zeus and Coyote). They also postulate a vast host of evil spirits who mean nothing but harm, for example, demons, devils, the jinn, bad winds, ghosts, and demiurges. These projections of human fear and hate into the supernatural realm fit Durkheim's view of religion as the collective representation of the community (Durkheim 1995 [1912]). These religious cultures of oppression heighten fear and hatred instead of promoting enlargement of the human spirit and connection to the divine.

Cultures of Despair

An important finding by Mirosław Kofta and his Polish coworkers (2020) demonstrates a strong and impressive causal link between feeling that politics and public life are out of one's control and susceptibility to believe hateful conspiracy theories. An example from this study is renewed Polish anti-Semitism. Feeling that social position and politics are spinning out of control is not just correlated but is actually causative in promoting hate. Although this study needs to be replicated for further data, it does fit very well with Albert Bandura's theory of self-efficacy (specifically the effects of lacking it; Bandura 1982), Baumeister's theory of endangered self-esteem, and other theories of good and evil. It may be explanatory for the fear and hatred of white supremacist groups in the United States against nondominant groups like Muslims and immigrants. Yu Ding and Krishna Savani (2020) have recently found that variability in phenomena ranging from weather, retail prices, and social strife makes people feel vulnerable and out of control, thus judging and wanting to publish wrongdoers more harshly.

Related to this is the work of Anne Case and Angus Deaton (2020) on deaths of despair. Case and Deaton have shown a very strong correlation of suicide, drug overdoses, and alcohol-related deaths. These in turn are related to health problems that can be caused by personal neglect, including poor diet. The problem has increased greatly over the twenty years among a very specific demographic: white males without college education. Deteriorating life conditions are part of it, but Case and Deaton point out that rapidly decreasing control over the situation is involved. Reliable employment, good wages, and stable supportive communities are all things of the past for most Americans in that demographic group.

This out-of-control sense of inequality and sheer bigness of powerful forces makes people feel weak, lacking in self-efficacy. Anger and hate are expressed as arrogance, racial superiority, and putting others down. Cowardice creates timidity and toxic conformity. Lost are the empowering cultural forms of art and literature, and even ordinary civility and decency. Weakness and fear make people desperate for security and respect. Cultures of despair respond to insecurity by becoming more defensive by becoming more violent.

SUMMARY

The roots of human evil are expressed in both individual variation and cultural constructs. When dictators whip up their populations to commit genocide, they must go beyond the individual and the culture. They must demand group loyalty, marginalizing and demonizing the "other." In chapter 6, we examine the exclusion of others.

Chapter 6

The Exclusion of Others

FAMILIES AND "OTHERING"

As a self-protective mechanism, infants are born with some innate fear of strangers, and the more different those strangers look and act from the parents, the more the fear. Thus, some degree of othering on the basis of appearance and voice sound is normal. On the other hand, infants show acute interest in other people, especially faces, toward which they orient (Tomasello 2019). They seem innately primed to recognize the more universal emotional expressions, for example, smiles and angry expressions. Infants react quickly to smiles, reassurance, gentle touch, and other marks of friendship, and react with fear to shouting and rapid, dramatic movement. They look to their parents for cues on how to react to a stranger. They are extremely reactive to parental moves and voices; the parents may be completely unaware of how strongly they are signaling the infant. Culture enters from early infancy, conditioning reactions. By age 3–4 years, children already know that certain recognizable groups are liked while others are disliked. They learn gender roles, clothing associated with gender, and other complex cultural messages, much learned unconsciously (Tomasello 2016, 2019).

Families train for culture-normative behavior, and prepare children to interact in the social sphere beyond the family level. Children are raised on stories explaining how to start or defuse a fight. This shaping reflects the values of the family and the language used is a definitive means by which families transmit these values. "Strict and nurturant family values explain individual differences in conservatism, liberalism, and the political middle" (Feinberg et al. 2020:777), with more strict families producing more conservative people, and conversely. This is a classic finding, applied to traditional hierarchies and religious purity societies. It is, however, only partially explanatory; other factors can change the outcomes.

Extensive analysis of Twitter tweets revealed that conservatives are more likely to use language related to "threat, power, tradition, resistance to change, certainly, security, anger, anxiety, and negative emotion in general," while liberals expressed more "benevolence." Crosscutting was a range from moderates to extremists on either side who were prone to use language expressing "inhibition, tentativeness, affiliation . . . anxiety . . . swear words, and death-related language" (Sterling et al. 2020:805). Conservatives did not stand out for conformity, attention to inequality, or anxiety, nor did liberals stand out for universalism, positive emotions, or self-direction (Sterling et al. 2020; note that since the meanings of "conservative" and "liberal" change over time, this finding may not apply outside of a specific context). Families are the kernel from which these values and resulting behavior are learned. Adolf Hitler, who status as a parent has never been definitively established, said of childrearing: "I want the young to be violent, domineering, undismayed, and cruel. . . . There must be nothing weak or gentle about them" (as quoted in Alice Miller 1983:142).

RIVALRY WITH "OTHERS"

Within the family, humans have occasional anger and aggression. Greater aggressiveness is usually targeted against rival groups outside of the family, however defined. Indifference is the reaction to most of the rest—the unknown multitudes outside the circle of one's immediate kin or threatening rivals. One consoling lie that people tell themselves is that we live in a just world, in which people get what they deserve (see Melvin Lerner 1980). The poor are poor because they are lazy, the rich are rich because they worked hard. Structural opponents, the "others," are unworthy and deserve what they get. Individuals and groups conforming to genocide often deeply believe in this world view: the others are truly monstrous, subhuman, totally the "other," the cause of all evil—callous, coldly planning aggression, and promoting bureaupathy.

The word "rival" literally means "sharer of a stream" (Latin *rivus*, stream), in recognition of the universality of arguments over water. As Mark Twain said, "Whiskey is for drinkin,' water's for fightin'" (attributed to Mark Twain). Rivalry is an excellent term to describe predictable reactions to structural opponent groups over water rights, power, land, jobs, social recognition, food, or any scarce resource. People tend to hold positive views of their own group and demean and feel rivalry with their opponents, especially when conflicts arise (Li and Leidner 2020). They may be hostile or minimizing toward rivals (infrahumanization), excluding others from *their own* circle. However, they may not necessarily hate them or exclude as part of humanity (Castano 2012; Leyens et al. 2000). Usually there is strong fear of rivals, especially in the face of salient conflicts (Kteily, Bruneau et al. 2015; Kteily, Hodson, and Bruneau 2016; Mann 2005; Parks and Stone 2010; Rovenpor et al. 2019). This often results in slanderous language—animal abuse terms such as cur, bitch, snake, rat, worm, cockroach, or terms referring to rivals as monsters, devils, machines, or automatons (Haslam 2006, 2020; Kteily, Bruneau et al. 2015). These insults succeed in distancing others but not in eliminating their humanity, since no one really thinks the rivals are worms or cockroaches (as Baumeister 1997 points out, one does not bother torturing real cockroaches slowly to death).

Beyond infrahumanization is dehumanization, the failure to define rivals as fully human or even human at all (Markowitz and Slovic 2020). This is a key component in conforming to genocide. Genocide authority Nick Haslam states, "The idea that dehumanization is an essential element in genocidal conflicts is now almost a truism, widely recognized by lay people and genocide scholars alike" (Haslam 2020:119). While hostility and minimizing result in infrahumanization, genocidal othering renders those outside of the reference group. They become Kantian objects (Kant 2002 [1785]): mere numbers on a spreadsheet, dirt to be bulldozed out of the way, underlings to be disregarded with callous indifference. Even when the other is conceded to have superior power, genociders negate their humanity and have exquisite knowledge of how to make them suffer pain and humiliation. David humiliates and kills the "giant" Goliath. From the Marquis de Sade to countless Hollywood script writers, dehumanization is coupled with pain and humiliation (see "Silence of the Lambs").

Dehumanization can be indirect, as when displacing people from their homes to build a dam, killing them via tobacco or toxic chemicals, or referring to them as "collateral damage" from a deadly drone from 10,000 miles away (Haslam 2020:134). Generally, the killers in these cases are not held accountable.

Structural Opponent Groups

In the United States, the classic structural opponents have been along lines of "race" and "diversity," defining the antagonism between blacks and whites. In Canada, structural opponents have been whites versus Native Americans (First Nations people). Blacks in the United States and First Nation people in Canada are notably overrepresented in "hard case" stories in the media—stories about substance abuse, crime, and welfare dependence—even where these minorities are a very small percentage of such cases. This is an example of inflicting pain and humiliation through systematic structural racism.

In most cultures, prejudices are camouflaged. To many American blacks, whites are suspect, racist, and dangerous. White racists may "hate" blacks but say they like their neighbors who happen to be black: "He isn't really a Black guy." One reason for such contradictions is the degree to which these structural opponent groups conform to local norms and morals. Typically, marginal groups are somewhat tolerated by mainstream society as long as they "keep their place" and do not try to assert rights. A racist who might tolerate an affable minority neighbor will not tolerate Al Sharpton. A misogynist may "love" and patronize his subservient wife but hate feminists. When ENA worked with fishermen in Hong Kong, he observed that they were regarded as lowly by most of society, but were tolerated as long as they did not assert equality in a stratified society and were normative in their behavior. When they asserted equality, which these tough sailors often did, there could be trouble.

A complex field experiment in twenty-eight German cities demonstrated the effects of normative behavior. There was considerable resistance to providing assistance to hijab-wearing women, but the same women without the hijab received little animosity compared to mainstream German women. In this field experiment hijab-wearing women participated in social protest against littering and were treated the same as non-hijab-wearing women. The hijab-wearing women were the researchers. The general conclusion was that persons different from mainstream society are tolerated if they concurrently mark their similarity by proactive, normative behavior (Choi et al. 2019).

Sometimes hard times bring people together and intergroup solidarity can promote cohesion (Greenaway and Cruwys 2019). However, difficult social and economic times can also exacerbate the otherness of structural opponents, for example, the large majority in the United States financially left behind watching the "one percent" get richer, both in the 1920s and now since 2016. Exclusion can be contingent upon a situation and who is defined as "other" can shift quickly. For instance, Muslims in the United States were basically ignored until 9/11, after which they were feared, stereotyped, and persecuted.

Religion as Rivalry and Othering

A common claim is that religious exclusion is the worst. Religion traditionally embodies the most basic values, hopes, dreams, and beliefs that people hold. Challenge to these basic features of society often threatens people more than any other form of challenge. The monotheistic "Abrahamic" religions have more narrowly exclusive interpretation than the religions of China and historic

Central Asia, where value-sets existed independent of religion (Biran 2005). An interesting observation is that those of any religion who practice the most extreme othering are often those who are not deeply knowledgeable about the tenets of their religion (compare Atran 2010 and Traverso 2019 on Islam with the highly inconsistent quotes from some Christian groups with limited knowledge of Biblical scholarship). More confusing still is a pattern, notable among some religious communities, for extreme tolerance of many kinds of behavior but extremely rigid observance of defining traditions of the group. Religion as a force for exclusion and othering may be based upon meaningless tags instead of content, as Edward Gibbon accused Christians of doing in the war over *homoousia* versus *homoiousia* (Gibbon 1995 [1776–1778], vol. 1, p. 787).

EXCLUSION OF FOLDBREAKERS

Humans everywhere dislike foldbreakers—people who conspicuously resist conforming to basic social rules. Even people who are saintly may be disliked because being so good is "different" (Parks and Stone 2010). While enforcing conformity may serve to make people comply, it can also create hatred for anyone who is conspicuously unlike the herd. Individuals (e.g., geniuses and artists) or groups (e.g., Jews in Christian countries, black people in white majority countries) who resist conformity may be especially targeted. Particularly in danger are highly salient "others" who are perceived as wealthier or more successful than dominant groups, such as Jews in Depression Europe, educated people in Cambodia in the 1970s, and Tutsi in Rwanda in the 1990s.

Dominant groups cope with foldbreakers by trying to convert them, ostracize them, or learning to tolerate them (Greenaway and Cruwys 2019), using cultural prescriptions for conflict resolution (Beals and Siegal 1966). If foldbreakers form a large enough faction to develop power, the dominant group, stressed and afraid of the competition, may be eroded by intragroup tension (Aalerding et al. 2018; Greenaway and Cruwys 2019). When the social pressures become overwhelming, intragroup deviants emerge (Greenaway and Cruwys 2019). If conflict mechanisms erode, the foldbreakers are simply killed (Wrangham 2019). If they survive, the members of these devalued groups may lose their sense of autonomy in proportion to the level of repression experienced (Kachanoff et al. 2019). They become less able to help themselves, precisely when they most need to do so.

Anthropologists have documented intolerance to deviance and consequent occasional breakup of communities among the Pueblo tribes of the southwestern United States, among small southeast European villages, and among Middle Eastern village societies.

SUMMARY

The common theme of exclusion is rejection of people simply for being what they are. Paul Farmer, physician and anthropologist, cofounder of Partners in Health, is quoted widely, "The idea that some lives matter less is the root cause of all that is wrong with the world." (See interview of Dr. Paul Farmer by Alvin Powell, Harvard Staff writer May 21, 2018. "To Be Horrified by Inequality and Early Death and Not Have Any Plan for Responding—That Would Not Work for Me." *The Harvard Gazette*, p. 7.)

We have had the privilege of talking with Dr. Farmer about this observation, which speaks to exclusion and otherness, whether judged to be very valuable or mattering less. It brings up the "toleration paradox": toleration is good, but tolerating intolerance is not, nor is toleration of abuse and harm. The real truth in Farmer's remark is that evil involves branding some people as undeserving of consideration. Prejudice—prejudging people, without looking at their realities—is the driving dynamic.

Critically important is awareness that there is a continuum from good to evil, and specifically from actual enmity to utterly unprovoked genocide: from treating people with antagonism, as enemies, because they actually are so, to treating them as enemies because they might really be a threat, to treating people as enemies because they seem different and numerous enough to seem a threat to fearful leaders, to treating any different group as a threat simply because its difference is obtrusive or because it is in the way of settlement or "development." This tends to correspond very closely with the continuum from courageous fighting against attacking force to increasingly cowardly displacement of aggression to ever weaker targets.

Group identification in humans is fluid, complex, and made within networks. Genociders work hard to divide people and set them against each other. Conversely, highlighting the degree to which targeted people are of one's own group leads to protecting them (Newman 2020, passim). During World War II, the U.S. government did everything possible to help mainstream Americans view Jews, blacks, and others as fellow Americans. This approach helped to decrease racial discrimination in the armed forces, although Japanese Americans did not fare so well. Part II explores the roots of human evil. Part III considers historical linkages of past and present to understanding the evolving patterns of conforming to genocide.

Part III

THE MARCH OF GENOCIDE

PAST AND PRESENT

"O heaven! that one might read the book of fate, and see the revolution of the times"

William Shakespeare
(*Henry IV* Part 2 Act III, scene 3)

Chapter 7

The Evolution of Genocide over Time

HUMAN EVOLUTIONARY PATTERNS

Human groups evolved primarily from patriarchal descents and fictive-ancestor lineages to sedentary agriculture with affiliation and association based upon place. This social phenomenon eventually led to the creation of nation-states with many societies becoming more matrilineal and tolerant of power-sharing with women. Since recorded history, there has been steady progress in science, arts, lifespan, food production, and health care. As complex large societies evolved, they needed markets, governance, and social norms to regulate political structures (Christian 2004; McNeill and McNeill 2003; Morris 2010; Turchin 2006, 2016). Making war has always been a part of the evolution of political structures.

More effort and resources have gone into making war than into almost any other sector of human action. Many technological innovations were developed for war, only later being adapted for peaceful civilian use. In the contemporary world, according to Pinker (2011), war and violent death are now less common than in early civilizations, although bloodier. However, Pinker exaggerates. Violent death rates have always been high (Wrangham 2019), ranging from less than 1 per 1,000 in peaceful modern societies to as many as 200 or more in some highly stressed tribes. While appearing to be less frequent (Pinker 2011; Wrangham 2019), wars in today's world are vaster in scope and genocide is a major cause of death. Global communication networks enable evil leaders to arouse group hate in ways not so easily managed in ancient societies.

TRENDS IN GENOCIDE OVER TIME

For countless millennia, people lived in small agrarian bands with little dif-
ferentiation except by age and gender (Boehm 1999). Antagonism and killing was directed primarily against rival clans, bandits, foreign "barbarians,"
and religious deviants. Tyrants killed political rivals and their families, but
destroying whole groups of nonoffensive subjects of one's *own* government
was not common, except in cases of religious crusades against "unbelievers"
and "heretics." These campaigns against "heretics," however, tended to spill
over into hate of "others," including hatred and murder of any weaker groups.

Targets changed over time. With the rise of complex societies arose inequitable hierarchies, exemplified by kings, emperors, and competition for
power. Warfare took place among rival claimants to the throne, and between
states, empires, ethnic groups, and religious factions. Large-scale killers were
often highly selective about their massacres. The Mongols and other Central
Asian conquerors, however, were famously indifferent to religion and even
ethnicity in their massacres; they were equal-opportunity killers of anyone
who resisted them. (Note, however, that the Mongol hordes rarely committed
genocide by our definition. They massacred only rivals who persisted in fighting back.) Over time, weak, corrupt regimes caused widespread discontent
and were dismantled (Ibn Khaldun 1958).

The ancient Greeks described a cycle of democracy, autocracy, tyranny,
collapse followed by democracy—all accompanied by killing. In Europe,
there was a trail of oppression and killing imposed by warring tribes and city-
states in the Roman Empire. After the fall of Rome, rival nobles assembled
cadres of knights and forced expendable peasants into service in wars of
religious hatred supporting political power. Conquered Persian dualists,
Jews, and Christians were all harassed and murdered in Roman Empire times
(Anderson 2019; Ibn Khaldun 1958).

After Constantine, Christians in the Roman Empire crushed non-Christians
and "heretics." Later, Europe, challenged by aggressive spread of trade, commerce, and new scientific knowledge from the Islamic world, resorted to the
crusades and persecution of heretics in the twelfth and thirteenth centuries.
Spain's Reconquista descended into genocide of both Muslims and Jews after
the final conquest of the Muslims in 1492. Then Europe's own progress and
religious ferment challenged old regimes in the sixteenth and seventeenth
centuries, leading to vast religious wars that involved genocidal murder of
opposing religious communities, for example, Irish Catholics in Ireland.
Later, the Treaty of Westphalia substituted nation-states for religious factions, and war became more a battle of nations than religion. Medieval and
early modern tyrants such as Philip the Fair, Ferdinand and Isabela, Oliver
Cromwell, Empress Dowager Cixi, Genghis Khan, and Zhu Yuanzhang

(the leader who drove the Mongols from China) represented elites against the forces of change, sometimes using genocidal strategies to advance their agendas.

In the nineteenth century, following the Industrial Revolution and its political revolutions, the forces of modernity rolled across the world. Some results were anti-Jewish pogroms, the persecution of serfs and minorities by Tsar Nicholas II in Russia, and the genocide of the Dzungars by the Qing Dynasty in China. In the early twentieth century, new ideas, arts, and sciences challenged primary production and Industrial Revolution strategies. Among the many positive post-Industrial Revolution strides were negative and corrosive factors—stagnant economies, unstable or inept governments, growing inequality, economic class division, racism, and militarism. These were critical historical factors leading to fascism and repression, the seeds of genocide.

HISTORICAL GENOCIDE DRIVERS

As Marx pointed out, "haves" versus "have-nots" is historically an opposition in society. Also, from the Assyrians to the European settlers of the Americas, and from the "barbarians" sacking Rome to the wars over oil in Africa in the 1980s and 1990s, acquiring loot has been a driver of war and genocide along with power grabs, religious hatred, and racism. In the centuries after the Industrial Revolution the seeds of genocide have sprouted—racism, ethnic hatred, economic class division, and imperialist colonialism leading to slavery, land grabs, and settler genocides. At the end of World War I, speaking to public complacency about these pervasive factors, William Butler Yeats wrote, "The best lack all conviction; the worst are full of passionate intensity" (*The Second Coming*, see Montague 1998: 238).

Racism as a visible, significant force began by the late Roman Empire, if not earlier, but was not a serious social factor until the sixteenth century, with the conquest of the Americas and much of Africa. The expansion of the slave trade drove racism to a high point in and after the eighteenth century. Plantation slavery and the slave trade were at their worst in the eighteenth century, and the reaction against them fueled the Enlightenment. The sugar plantations of the Caribbean created a level of horror almost unprecedented in the world (Beckford 1972; Mintz 1985; Stedman 1988 [1790]). It was often easier and less expensive to buy new enslaved Africans than to keep enslaved workers alive, so starvation and disease caused enormous mortality. The production was entirely for export, not for local consumption, so there was no need to preserve a local economy, or pay any workers well. The plantation owners were in a virtual—and sometimes literal—state of war against their enslaved workers (Stedman 1988 [1790]). The conflict of plantation owners and servile workers is a large part of the back story of the conflictual relationship of the fossil fuel and military-industrial complexes with humanity today, and presents a simple model for it.

The historical record attests that one can predict with considerable accuracy the amount of evil in society by assessing the nature of rentier or primary-production-firm dominance of the political economy and the level of militarism. Societies dependent on large-scale plantations worked by servile labor have a particularly bloody record. So do conflict-torn marginal and poorly controlled agrarian states. A contemporary contrast compares Afghanistan and Bhutan, both equally agrarian. Afghanistan, rampant with landlordism and steeped in a heritage of violence from the days of Alexander the Great, compares with peaceable and relatively equitable Bhutan. Another example is the conversion of formerly warlike societies to currently peaceful ones, such as the Scandinavian nations. The United States is an example of a nation currently struggling with lingering racism and power abuses grounded in plantation slavery and genocide of Native Americans.

POSITIVE HISTORICAL TRENDS

Following the observations of Adam Smith (1910/1776) and other political economists, there are some positive historical trends protecting against genocide. In economies dominated by rentier-owned primary production—agribusiness, mining, fossil fuels, and the like—evil leaders are able to exploit a politically weak population and amass vast wealth. This exploitation creates a regressive and often repressive society. Agrarian societies from the Inca to Sumer to China all wound up structurally the same: city, king, court, bureaucracy, dominating vast agrarian populations with little wealth. At least, those rural populations had genuine agricultural knowledge and skills. More recent rentier economies are worse, hiring (or enslaving) unskilled labor, paid little or nothing, from economically stagnant regions. Inversely, there has been gradual recognition globally that expanding economies, especially those dominated by trade and commerce, must invest in human resources. The innovations developed by the workforce are critical to economic survival.

Innovation has spread from rich cores of trade and communication-based systems. Military technology seems to spread fastest of all innovations. Next come innovations in communication; people deeply desire to be in touch. Then comes ordinary production. Primary production still dominates most of the world's surface area.

Progress has occurred, fitfully, throughout history, despite long declines like that of the Roman Empire. In the seventeenth century, rationalized property rights and freer markets were followed by the influence of the Enlightenment upon law and recourse, ideals of free speech, press, religion, assembly, and conscience. An emerging premise was that all societies have three processes operating: negative feedback loops maintaining the situation without change, cycles of change, and positive feedback loops producing slow progress or decline over time. Equality before the law for full citizens, and expansion of the citizen concept, came a bit later in the eighteenth century. This change in social thinking led, under Quaker influence, to the discussion of abolition of slavery. As a social system, however, slavery was not eliminated until the nineteenth century in almost every part of the world, and (as noted above) is not totally gone yet. The fact that the Enlightenment coincided with the worst excesses of imperialism and slavery is all too well known, but does not vitiate Enlightenment goals; they were developed explicitly to counteract those unsavory developments.

A key to the success of the Enlightenment was the development of world trade too rapid for any nation-state to control it. As opportunity exploded, traders managed international networks, dealing with minimal government supervision and working with huge differences in cultures, faiths, and technologies. This was one breeding ground for the emergence of concepts of liberty, self-governance, tolerance, freedom of conscience, and personal responsibility. One can compare the rapid rise of the Enlightenment ideas in multinational Europe with its relative failure in East Asia during the centuries when the Qing Dynasty imposed its crushing weight on the East Asian world-system. The Enlightenment did not invent the rule of law or welfare-oriented governments; Europe and China already had those. What the Enlightenment brought were science and participatory democracy coupled with the ideal of freedom of conscience. The historical tendency to repress the masses was countered by the power of the education. A key positive outgrowth was the initiation of free public education, an idea springing from the early nineteenth century.

Responding to these pivoting changes were the writing of the American Founding Fathers. They worked with a strong sense that we are all in this together and that my rights stop where yours start, sometimes phrased as "your right to swing your arm ends at my nose." They were keenly aware that a society, its laws, and its economic wellbeing exist within a moral shell. It is universally true of high ideals that mere fallible humans have trouble following them. Based upon the thinking of John Locke and Adam Smith, the U.S. Constitution embodies these principles, giving rise to a system emphasizing freedom of conscience, speech, religion, ideology, assembly, and voting. It also incorporated free enterprise within reason, freedom from torture, warrantless search, and other abuses of government power. It meant equality in justice, opportunity, and law, with protection in oppression. It meant rule of law, not of capricious rulers. It meant presumption of innocence, protection of all, and mutual defense. These were seen as necessary because evil so often wins unless actively stopped. In America, this is a work in progress—a long experiment in learning to live by the values so hopefully stated and so imperfectly followed. The arc of justice and civil rights followed, bringing inspirational, while imperfect, justice and individual protection.

SUMMARY

Today, with closing frontiers, these ideals are under siege. Many of the poor have given up hope of getting rich; they can only hope to cut other, weaker groups down and take what little those groups have. This is a negative-sum game. Some cultures are much more prone to see the world as a zero-sum or negative-sum game than are others (Różycka-Tran et al. 2015; Stavrova and Ehlebracht 2016). The United States was formerly rather moderate in this regard, but zero-sum and negative-sum thinking has increased.

The normal human tendency to weather down and adapt to the system was always used by the elites to repress the masses. During the last three centuries, a typical course of progress ran thus (McNeill and McNeill 2003; Morris 2010). A few idealists will see a problem and a solution. If they have a voice and if the problem gets worse, more and more people will be attracted to the cause, until a majority is on board and can prevail.

In the United States, the values of the Enlightenment slowly extended over time. Slavery was a major crisis: antislavery rhetoric was early dismissed as crackpot thinking, but with the progressive damage to the whole U.S. economy by plantation agriculture and its enslaved workers, antislavery thinking prevailed. Next came mounting criticism of deforestation and wildlife loss in the late nineteenth century, climaxing in Theodore Roosevelt's environmental reforms. Then came the Great Depression, which led to massive economic reforms, followed by vigorous (though ultimately inadequate) response to the environmental and food production crises in the 1960s and early 1970s.

Visionaries are always proposing new reforms, but these are picked up by the majority only if they are perceived as practical ways of addressing real and worsening problems. Deteriorating conditions allow the visionaries to lead in many measures that the majority would probably not support otherwise. The Bill of Rights, for instance, was added to the Constitution by Enlightenment visionaries; the Bill probably went beyond what the majority wanted at the time. Crises after independence were caused by the reactionary behavior of the plantation and big-firm sectors. This chapter has considered historical linkages from the past contributing to and preventing genocide. Chapter 8 examines contemporary patterns that protect against and contribute to conforming to genocide.

Chapter 8

Present Darkness

THE COLLAPSE OF TRADITIONAL SOCIETY

Francis Fukuyama, famed for his overoptimistic views of the future, has now acknowledged the present darkness, the national and global sense of gloom (2016). This darkness did not suddenly happen. It occurred in parallel with profound cultural changes in the twentieth and twenty-first centuries. In traditional agrarian society, life was short and frequently ended violently. People often escaped into religion, or spirit power, to manage uncontrollable forces and to receive hope. They relied upon songs and folk literature to remind them that their lives mattered—that life and death need not be in vain. The work ethic spoke to hard work, cooperation, and toughness in the face of adversity. This world had its wonderful side, but it also had its own darkness—racism, religious bigotry, class oppression, and gender biases, often silently endured.

Now the traditional world of rural villages across the world and small-town America is gone or fading. This world of churches, temples, village mosques, local folksingers, cottage industry, and the family farm is dissolving as hi-tech and smart machines replace workers and farming everywhere. The economic underpinning of production has become concentrated in a few corporate hands. One of the first casualties of this shift has been is the disappearance of a grounded sense of community (Putnam 2000).

The decline of traditional culture after 1950 led to the emergence of "popular" culture and thirst for material consumption. For many youths, video games and comic books have replaced time spent studying the arts and the literary classics. Many others worldwide have taken refuge in increasingly defensive religiosity. In America, older workers have watched from the sidelines as their job skills were replaced by automation and their "white" privilege was challenged by upwardly mobile minorities. Life is frustrating, especially for those who are not succeeding as well as they expected.

In the 1960s, burgeoning interest in traditionally nonwestern introspective religions quickly faded, as did the humanistic psychology and personal development movements of the 1970s. A backlash of defensive individuals trying to appear competent in the face of "self-improvement" evolved. Some pertinent examples of this cultural roller coaster included the hope that men would "talk about feelings." This hope collapsed as men policed each other with the classic "suck it up" and "be tough" lines. Women trying to "do it all," that is, succeeding in the hard-scrabble career world, raising perfect children, and being the ideal spouse, became exhausted or angry. The hope that people could deal with their problems in the absence of the folk communities led to alienation and fear. This was a factor leading to fascism in Europe in the 1920s and 1930s, and has continued to be a key determinant in growing global fascism today. Far-right movements across the world have used this trend to unite followers in fear, bigotry, and hatred, providing debasing entertainment (video games, trash music, social media hate sites). They are the henchmen of hate leading to genocide in this present time. George Orwell (1950) foresaw all these trends and commented extensively on them in his essays. It was a "not so brave" world (to play on Aldous Huxley's *Brave New World*, 1932), as social changes shaped identity politics in the new millennium.

THE RISE OF GIANT CORPORATIONS

As folk society and traditional elite society collapsed with the decline of local communities and the rise of mass society (Putnam 2000), people became more and more dependent on giant corporations to integrate their worlds. Politics became less public and more corporate. Lateral, community association shifted to top-down hierarchies. Globally, the steady rise of giant firms has had a distorting effect on the economy, politics, and culture (Anderson 2010; Anderson and Anderson 2013, 2017; Piketty 2017; Putnam 2000; Snyder 2018; Turchin 2016). Face-to-face community has been largely replaced by virtual communities. Among the casualties are newspapers, local helpfulness, and bowling leagues. Robert Putnam's book *Bowling Alone* (2000) used the decline of bowling leagues as a marker of decline of civic culture in America, a collapse into Tocquevillian "subjects" as opposed to "citizens," as Putnam put it. The result is despair as lack of civility, economic and social stress, drug overdoses, suicide, and other markers of despair increase.

The horrors of the Great Depression and World War II evolved into a "lullaby culture," the soothing pop culture of the early 1950s, creating an increasingly homogeneous culture via expanding mass communication.

Entertainment was defined as watching TV, movies, or later playing video games. Children migrated indoors, abandoning much of imaginative childhood to spending hours passively entertained and growing fat. The arts succumbed to dominance by giant "entertainment" corporations, dominated by faddism and conformity. Life settled on the least emotionally and cognitively involving forms: pop art, fast food, mindless music, and anti-intellectualism. These cultural changes initially fit very well with the agendas of many giant firms.

Those corporations using "sunsetting" production processes, like fossil fuel extraction, have harmed humans and the environment. Especially damaging are big oil, big coal, toxic chemicals, big tobacco, and the munitions-arms-military procurement industries (Kirby 2017). They flourish by polluting, selling guns, resisting clean power, digging up mountains, and often damaging the public interest. They have funded much of the fear, hatred, war, and antiscience activity of the past few decades (Anderson and Anderson 2013; Auzanneau 2018; Mayer 2016). As such, they have contributed to the global trends in war and genocide.

"Big oil" and "big coal" were once the very definition of progress, lionized and esteemed even as they underpaid their workers badly and subjected them to harsh working conditions. Now these large extraction firms are victims of progress, rapidly being sidelined by the rise of clean efficient energy, the information highway, the attacks on their practices by the scientific community, shifts in cultural thinking about environmental destruction, and the popular media—all promoting a more ecologically sane world. "Big agriculture," chemically dependent and increasingly controlling the food system, is likewise distrusted. The tobacco industry has demonstrated reactionary but clever strategies to cope with the public concern: deny and cover up scientific findings as long as possible, expand markets to vulnerable, poor nations, lobby for government protection and subsidies, and intensively market emerging products while cultivating a new generation of users. A key example is the adolescent vaping epidemic. The fossil fuels and chemical industries learned, and have copied these tactics with enthusiasm and with millions of dollars expended (Hope 2019; Michaels 2008, 2020; Oreskes and Conway 2010). These strategies, for the most part, have worked.

Government Support of Giant Firms

Government support of giant corporations is global in scope. It is an economic form developed during the 1930s. Hitler adhered to the idea as part of "national socialism." In China and some other socialist countries, giant primary-production firms are part of the government structure, not separate entities. Giant corporations depend heavily upon subsidies and special favors to thrive financially. Fossil fuels receive over $649 billion in federal subsidies in the United States every year (Ellsmoor 2019 per the International Monetary Fund). As the large sunsetting industries become more threatened, their need to apply for government subsidies becomes paramount. They lobby for tax breaks, seek increased subsidies, design sophisticated public relations strategies, and hire more lawyers (Johnston 2007; Kummer 2018; Michaels 2008, 2020; Oreskes and Conway 2010). Big oil would not be financially viable without government support, because the costs of cleaning up pollution and dealing with damages would be insupportable (Oil Change International 2017). Without government protection, many CEOs could be in danger of imprisonment for deliberate release of pollution.

Related to subsidies are concessions that desperate cities and nations offer to giant firms as enticement to set up business in their jurisdictions. For example, Elon Musk convinced the State of Nevada to provide $1.3 billion to support the start-up of a battery plant. Jeff Bezos asked New York City for $3 billion for a new eastern headquarters of Amazon. The offer was refused. Bezos eventually settled for $762 million from the State of Virginia (Soper et al. 2020). These kinds of favors amount affect taxpayers in two ways: the taxpayers pay for the "gifts" and they lose government services that may be cut as a result. The claim that these firms will produce wealth for the community in the form of taxes and wages rarely materializes. For example, cutting down tropical rain forests in Central America for cattle development by giant multinational corporations has resulted not only in massive loss of forest and low-impact subsistence farming, but also shift of agrarian population to urban slums, job loss, hunger, and erosion of child health (Grandia 2012; McSweeney et al. 2014; Stonich 1993). The meat was imported to the United States and Central American children went hungry.

The Influence of Giant Firms on Government Agendas

Increasingly, stressed, sunsetting giant corporations are at odds with the needs of populations and sustainable environments. Financial aggregation is often given priority over human and ecological systems. To keep the subsidy line open, a substantial portion of subsidy funding is funneled into political donations, effectively bribing legislators. They fund government and nongovernmental organizations that support their agendas and protect their positions. They seek to merge corporations and government. This is a pattern characteristic of the end phases of political cycles trending toward instability. It is characterized by explosive increase in rent-seeking, shady financial dealings, and economic inefficiency (Mazzucato 2018). Corruption and white-collar crime increase as enforcement of laws weakens or ceases (Hobbes 2020).

In the case of the United States, much corporate money is invested in antiscience propaganda necessary for the continuation of giant firms, such as denial of global warming or the deleterious effects of tobacco. They sow doubts about the value and truthfulness of science (Michaels 2008, 2020; Oreskes and Conway 2010). They encourage racism by supporting white supremacist agendas advancing a repressive, intolerant environment (Phillips 2006). As such they contribute to fear, hatred, and the road to genocide. Examples in the United States include the great oil barons such as the Koch brothers, who funded global warming denial as well as the Tea Party, ALEC, and other right-wing agendas, including armed demonstrations (Abrams 2015; Auzanneau 2018; Cahill 2017; Folley 2019; Heinberg 2017; Hope 2019; Klein 2007, 2014; Leonard 2019; Mayer 2016; Nesbit 2016; Ross 2012; Wenar 2016). Koch money funded many or most of the attacks on civil rights and African American causes in recent decades. Many of these references detail the enormous sums paid to congresspersons for special favors. Even more extreme are the Mercers, who fund the major white supremacist and far-right hatred organizations and media (Gertz 2017; Silverstein 2018; Timmons 2017), and the Princes, the family of Secretary of Education Betsy DeVos and indicted mercenary fighter Erik Prince. Heavily dependent upon federal subsidies, contracts, sweetheart deals, loopholes, giveaways, and failure to enforce laws, these firms have the most to lose if the government centers upon the citizens rather than the profits. Thus, support leadership from a government that furthers their agenda. The Trump administration installed leadership in the environmental agencies from oil, coal, agrochemical, and related polluting and environment-damaging industries (Friedman and O'Neill 2020).

Some of the most powerful giant firms have been successful in dividing the voters to eliminate any chance of unity against the common threat that fossil fuels present. Big oil, and especially the Koch interests, has spread their tentacles throughout the world. Najib Ahmed, writing in *Le Monde diplomatique*, shows "US climate deniers are working with far-right racists to hijack Brexit for Big Oil," which "exemplifies how this European nexus of climate science denialism and white supremacism is being weaponized by US fossil fuel giants with leverage over Trump's government" (Ahmed 2019 https://mondediplo.com/outsidein/brexit-climate-deniers). This pattern is seen globally. The United States, Russia, Turkey, Brazil, and others are now trapped. They depend financially upon a handful of giant corporations, their own or foreign, that are increasingly acting against the interests of the populace and use influence and bribery for support, including exemption from laws, especially those protecting people against physical damage. Pollution and global warming are killing millions worldwide, because of this deadly connection. For example, China's tobacco industry operates with the full support of the government, although tobacco kills 1.2 million Chinese a year. The government depends on tobacco taxes and many individual politicians depend on bribes (Kohrman et al. 2018).

In this present darkness, the rise of strongmen—individuals who specifically and explicitly violate laws and morals to show they are above such things—has promoted the rise of fascist leaders feeding on hate. We see this trend across the world—Hungary, India, Israel, Kazakhstan, Myanmar, Philippines, Poland, Russia, Sri Lanka, Turkmenistan, Uganda, the United States, and elsewhere. Juntas with similar amoral characteristics, but lacking the strongman image, control another few dozen nations. Strongmen sometimes limit themselves to military dictatorship (as currently in Egypt) but more often invoke full-scale fascist regimes, with ethnic hatred, fusion of government and giant corporations, militarism, glorification of force, and other fascist principles. They are skilled at mobilizing otherwise peaceful, passive majorities against minorities. This pattern has precedent in ancient records: Nebuchadnezzar, many Roman emperors, and conquerors such as Tamerlane and Henry VIII. Today's strongmen sanction their rule by appeals to extremist religion or its ideological equivalent (especially communism). This extremism is virtually identical, whether called "Christian," "Muslim," "Jewish," "Buddhist," or "socialist." It sanctions total power in the hands of the ruler; repression of women, often to the point of rendering them passive vessels of men; violence in defense of the faith; denial of equal rights to the "other"; and opposition to the messages of peace, love, harmony, forgiveness, and charity that are the hallmarks of these faiths. Strongmen lead violent attacks on weaker minorities and the "others," whether political, ethnic, religious, or lifestyle (MacLean 2017).

POLITICAL AGENDAS HELD HOSTAGE IN THE TWENTIETH AND TWENTY-FIRST CENTURIES

Currently in the United States, the Republican Party has been captured by donations from giant sunsetting corporations. It is the vehicle for subsidizing big oil, big coal, big agribusiness, and the military procurement and arms industry including provision of weapons to allies (Cahill 2017). Huge subsidies and special favors for giant corporations are now the rule, in a climate of corruption. It has become a party of white supremacy and military right-wing fundamentalist Christian agitation (Anderson 2017; Lauter 2019). The Democrats have moved from the party of the working class into the party of relatively upwardly mobile groups: minorities, women, urban young people, education and health care groups, and to some extent the hi-tech world. This new party alignment gives Republicans a perfect platform to mobilize scapegoating and repression and the Democrats to be cornered in defensiveness (Green 2017).

Historically, this party alignment was not the pattern. In the broad contours of U.S. politics in the early twentieth century, Republicans were the party of business, ranging from family farms to local businesses and up to large firms; Democrats were the party of labor. This led to reasonable dialogue (despite some bullying and cruelty). The change beginning in the 1920s, but not serious till the 1970s, was toward a Republican Party uniting racism and giant reactionary firms, and eventually a Democratic Party that became absorbed with identity politics more than with economic issues. This has led to negativity, division, hatred, racism, religious bigotry, and extremism. Political discussion of economic issues is increasingly contaminated or lost in a welter of mutual accusations. As Mahatma Gandhi supposedly said, "An eye for an eye makes the whole world blind" (attributed to Gandhi though actually not recorded among his words).

Political activism peaked in the 1930s and again in the 1960s with the worker movements, civil rights, and antiwar protests. Utopian experiments such as communes expressed hope but disintegrated. The 1960s got many people motivated, but solidarity movements, voter drives, demonstrations, teach-ins, and other forms of resistance thinned out as the twentieth century moved toward the millennium. The Great Depression and World War II solidified the whole nation around political progress toward the good, but the momentum could not last.

One casualty of the political trends in the later twentieth century has been the loss of traditional conservatism, a coalition of small-government and pro-environment advocates and defenders of law and order. Once characterized by a strong sense of honor and honesty, they have been co-opted into movements of hatred and extremism. The attitude toward the environment has been reversed, as extensively documented by Turner and Isenberg (2018); conservatives and Republicans in general had generally championed conservation in the early twentieth century (think of Theodore Roosevelt), but the GOP has become more and more antienvironment, reaching an extreme under Trump. The current "conservatives" favor the rights of giant firms to disrupt and damage the environment (Popovich et al. 2020). They support big government interfering in people's private lives, that is, reproductive choice, sexual orientation, and religious preference. They support strongmen and are not troubled by covert deals with nations against America's interests, for example, with Russia, Saudi Arabia, and North Korea.

Between 1970 and 2016, profound political changes occurred in voting allegiance. For example, the border South, Idaho, Montana, and the Dakotas shifted from previously liberal thinking to isolationist conservatism, parallel with the decline of labor unions and small family farms. As the giant primary-production firms expanded and assumed more power in those states, there was a steady stream of right-wing propaganda telling people that their problems were not due to economic unfairness or mismanagement but to rather to minorities. Messages of hate blamed minorities rather than a system of inequity. The sheer number of "others" attacked by the Republicans in the 2016 and 2018 campaigns was comparable to the tactics of Hitler and Stalin in mobilizing hatred and ostracism. Muslims, Latin Americans, non-Christians, LGBTQ persons, environmentalists, liberals, and many other groups were subjected to uncompromising rhetoric.

Surveys reported a massive voting flip, especially in 2016, from voting self-interest to voting against the "other." Investigative journalism (Mayer 2016; Rich 2018) described the enmeshment between giant firms and the new Republican stance on government—a long-standing network of friendship, political aid, mentorship, and power-sharing, going directly back to the pro-Hitler Koch and Coors family interests in the 1930s. These investigations revealed that Donald Trump was tied directly to McCarthy's right-hand man, Roy Cohn; that the Koch brothers started the Tea Party and other right-wing organizations (Checks and Balances Project 2017). All are connected by personal and financial ties.

Trump voters have their reasons for their angst, as analyzed by Bob Azarian in *Psychology Today* (2019). They perceive declining morality in the nation, fear change, and express hatred of the "other." Exaggeration and lies by Republicans and racial and ethnic slanders by Trump have contributed to targeted hatred toward immigrants and Muslims. Trump's core followers include neo-Nazis, white supremacists, and religious extremists, but also traditional Republicans (well-to-do suburbanites and business owners). He also has attracted blue-collar workers from the rural and small-town "rust-belt" world where physical strength and skill are often valued over intellect. Many have firm local loyalties that do not relate well to globalization and place high value on honesty, honor, and hard work. They would normally loathe individuals like Trump and his message, but they are hurt by a world that is passing them by and demeaning them as "rednecks." Trump has turned out to be a stunningly effective leader of groups that felt they were dominant, are now challenged, and are aggrieved and worried. He received enthusiastic support of white supremacists, religious groups opposing civil and reproductive rights, big oil firms threatened by ecological activism, less educated older whites threatened by the rise of educated youth, rural and rust-belt voters, the submissive women socialized to male orientation, and others who felt left out by a changing world. Their fears are sometimes real. Immigrants who tend to be highly motivated and enterprising do present a threat to the job security and social status of these groups, as do upwardly mobile women and minorities when freed from discriminatory hiring (Mutz 2018).

The right-wing media, for example, Fox News, has deliberately incited many middle-of-the-road people into hate, fueling incivility, as described by Lilliana Mason in her book *Uncivil Agreement* (2018). Giant corporations profit from redirecting outrage against economic injustice against feared minorities. They support Fox News, Breitbart, Sinclair, and their equivalents in other countries, rapidly escalating hatred of all sorts. Trump has mocked and distained "others" while sending messages of divisiveness and revolt against public safety, for example, "Liberate Minnesota" during the Covid-19 pandemic demonstrations. Instead of bringing people together in a changing world, these forces have substituted fear and hatred and animated many a weak soul who calls out opponents as "weak" or "snowflakes." Conspiracy theories multiply (Barkun 2013).

Such callousness justifies over $700 billion a year for "defense"—military adventuring—and $649 billion in subsidies to the giant fossil fuel corporations, while claiming the United States "cannot afford" medical care for all or food for the hungry. It follows the ideology of Nietzsche glorifying power and mass murder during the Nazi regime. In short, the political conditions for genocide are very real in the United States and in more than a dozen other countries. The only hope lies in lawful restraint of government and of private forces that collude to abuse power, while at the same time creating opportunities for economic and social progress.

CURRENT DESPAIR AND ANTI-INTELLECTUALISM: AN ERA OF ANTI-ENLIGHTENMENT

Anti-Enlightenment is the theme of this era, as giant reactionary corporations mobilize the forces of obscurantism. The "alt-right," extreme with strongly white supremacist views, has mobilized neofascists, racists, extreme nationalists, and similar persons. They are marked by extreme distrust of mainstream media. About 6 percent of Americans self-describe themselves as alt-right (Forscher and Kteily 2020). They strongly support Donald Trump. However, such extreme and narrow positions are not confined to the right wing. A new puritanism—divisive, identity-obsessed, and opposed to Jurgen Habermas' ideas of civil discourse and accommodation (Habermas 1987)—has spread from the right to the left. A substantial percentage of "progressives" are narrow and intolerant in their own ways, strongly rejecting centrist and moderate positions and sometimes demonstrating strongly antiwhite attitudes (such attitudes are by no means confined to nonwhites). The case is familiar to some of us who went through the 1960s: seeing the other side of the same coin, not realizing that the coin itself—confrontation, judgmentalism, and narrowness—is the problem.

All the worst things that progressives and liberals feared over the last fifty years came together in a perfect storm in the Trump administration, which attacked democracy, freedom, equality before the law, the environment, science, minorities, the press, the poor, the workers. One main driver has been the rise of inequality—especially the rise in power and wealth of the rich. The rich are literally above the law; it is almost impossible to convict them of anything, given their ability to pay lawyers and bribe politicians. A complex of five deadly ideas has become established by the Trump administration and the GOP. Trump encourages his followers to believe any convenient lies rather than the truth, and demonizes science. This feeds group solidarity against perceived challengers. Trump then models defiant irresponsibility, as in the opening-up movement and not wearing a mask during the Covid-19 epidemic. All this leads to the final and worst idea: we—our group—can survive and flourish only by increasingly harsh and disproportionate repression of weaker groups.

Nazism and fascism have been revived, with even more focus on Big Lies than in Hitler's Germany. Right-wing rallies are now a sea of Confederate and Nazi flags. Trump is directly copying Hitler; veteran civil rights lawyer Burt Neuborne has listed eleven pages of close, highly specific similarities (Neuborne 2019:22–33). Trump kept Hitler's speeches by his bed for years (Neuborne 2019:20), and sometimes uses Hitler's literal words. The Big Lie and other fascist methods of control and role are manifestations of weak fear. Since 2016 they have become the government. Nor is the United States unique; this is a worldwide movement (Luce 2017; Snyder 2018).

The worst of that process is that it allows truly evil people, who are often motivated by extreme greed and hate, to get ahead. Contrary to tropes of "the 1%," most rich people are reasonable enough, though perhaps motivated to be relatively conservative. The problem is that the few evil rich—the Kochs, Mercers, Princes, Trumps, and their ilk—are highly motivated to seek power. Since they are ruthless, they outcompete others. When they get power, they use it vindictively. They do not merely increase their wealth; they attack the body politic. Current problems in the United States include a full-scale frontal attack on democracy: on free press, voting rights, civil rights, civility, and equal protection under the law. Brian Klaas, in his book *The Despot's Apprentice* (2017), provides a thorough account of these attacks, with many important and thought-provoking comparisons to tyrannies and despotisms around the world.

Republican proposals to limit labor unions, roll back civil rights protection, cut funding for public education, suppress as many voters as possible, especially minorities, gerrymander states, eliminate environmental protection, and limit freedom to protest have made enormous headway in Republican-controlled states and even nationally. The Koch family has been proposing and funding most of this, establishing and supporting groups from the Tea Party to the Heritage Foundation (Mayer 2016). Proposals to eliminate Social Security and Medicare, as well as "Obamacare," are at play in Congress.

The war on science and public truth has become more serious as the Trump administration gained increasing control of departments and agencies, censored speech, cut funding for science, and denied scientific facts (Friedman 2017; Michaels 2020; Sun and Eilperin 2017; Tom 2018). Many Republicans have come to hate and fear education, especially higher education; polls show that most oppose and distrust it (Savransky 2017). The few giant firms that support right-wing politics to the tune of hundreds of millions of dollars a year now control the United States through the Republican Party. The 2017 tax cuts, opposed by 75 percent of voters and appealing only to the rich, show this dominance clearly. Democracy is suffering from increasing distortion (Browning 2018). Democracy and freedom in the United States are threatened, unless Americans unite to save their best traditions (Anderson and Anderson 2017; Klaas 2017).

There is despair as justice is corrupted at the highest levels (Eisinger 2017; Neuborne 2019) and racism and religious prejudice, financed by giant firms, are taking over politics (Beauchamp 2018; Lopez 2017; MacLean 2017; Metzl 2019). From the farthest right, there are calls for civil war and mass killings (Nova 2017). The health and wellbeing of Americans is deteriorating. Life expectancy has decreased, maternal mortality has steadily increased, and the health of infants and children is among the lowest in the developed world (National Research Council and the Institute of Medicine 2013). American children are 70 percent more likely to die before reaching age twenty-one than children in other developed countries; high infant mortality and enormous levels of gunshot deaths are the main causes (Kliff 2018; National Research Council and the Institute of Medicine 2013). Americans women have the highest mortality rate during childbearing of any developed country, higher even than the rate in some economically transitional nations (Amnesty International 2011; Anderson and Roberts 2019; MacDorman and Declercq 2018).

Suicides and deaths from alcohol and opiate abuse abound, strongly correlated geographically to high Trump voting. These conditions of despair are especially high levels in rural counties in Appalachia, the northern Midwest, and downwardly mobile areas (Case and Deaton 2015, 2020; Hayes et al. 2018; Policytensor 2019; Snyder 2018). Since these areas are overwhelmingly ethnic white, much of the despair translates into anger against minorities who are supposedly taking their livelihoods or at least their white privilege. Diana Mutz (2018) found that voting for Trump tracked perceived threats to group status more than economic woes.

Many people of the younger generation now appear to be in despair, giving up and saying that this discordance has always been the pattern in America. They point to a bloody history of slavery, genocide of Native Americans, internment of Japanese, Jim Crow laws, denial of the vote to women, the institutionalized harassment of Mexicans and Mexican Americans by the Texas Rangers, antigay violence, and ICE abuse of immigrants on the southern U.S. border with Mexico, and much more. However, those ills have always been challenged or are currently being challenged. Many have eventually been stopped through widespread public support and heroic efforts. Slavery was stopped by a bloody war. The movements for women's suffrage, fair labor laws, and civil rights prevailed in the end.

Even so, there is still abuse of "others." An economic downturn or fear of losing the 2020 elections could precipitate dictatorship and its inevitable result (Neuborne 2019). The Covid-19 pandemic with huge loss of life and economic viability presents a major threat. It is possible that the Republican administration will crack down, declare a state of emergency, suspend the Constitution, and begin full-scale genocide (Anderson and Anderson 2017; Goitein 2019). The centrists, liberals, and moderate-conservatives of the United States have very little time to unite and stop this. Without unity, it is unstoppable. The far-right has stalwart unity in their messages of fear and hatred while centrist and the progressives are assuming a position of being "the opposition"—often opposing rather than proposing.

Systemic structural racism, religious bigotry, and antiscience rhetoric merged into outright violence in 2020, with defiance of Covid-19 social distancing, opportunistic rioting and looting pursuant to peaceful demonstrations against police killings of black persons, and pervasive right-wing violence and threats. There is a real fear of autocratic takeover. A totalitarian regime in the United States would certainly turn to genocide (the predictor variables described in chapter 1 leave no doubt), with LGBTQ people and liberal leaders among the targets.

SUMMARY

Part III has explored historical and contemporary patterns that protect against and contribute to conforming to genocide. Part IV examines the duality of the good and bad wolf in our contemporary landscape, tensions of fear and hatred, tolerance and acceptance, and divisiveness from genocidal leaders. Finally, we offer some visionary thoughts on how to feed the good wolf, to play to the better side of our human nature.

Part IV

WHICH WOLF WILL WE FEED?

"If you can look into the seeds of time, and say which grain
will grow and which will not, speak then unto me"

William Shakespeare
(*Macbeth*, Act 1 Scene 3)

Chapter 9

Vulnerability to Conformity

LEARNING WHICH WOLF TO FEED

We now return to the analogy of the wolf you feed, a metaphor of choice between good and evil. The good wolf is fed on the kibble of kindness; the bad wolf on a diet of fear and hate. Deciding which wolf to feed is learned in childhood, a systematic, long-term, mentored process from simple to complex, concrete to abstract. Children start with a unique, innate bundle which is molded in an environmental and epigenetic milieu. Families create the basic psychodynamics. Children learn behavior and coping strategies from their parents, in particular, ways of dealing with stress and fear. The peer group affects this learning and provides the ways to express those dynamics (Harris 1998). Culture is the medium in which models are learned. Individual experiences in childhood explain part of adult behavior.

Individual innate characteristics and upbringing predisposes adaptation—some ways are learned quickly, others resisted, but in the end almost everyone conforms to the norms they are taught from their culture. "Deviations from expected social behavior are experienced as a threat to one's social identity, leading to punishment of those seen as violating cultural expectations regarding socially proper behavior" (Voorhees et al. 2020:194). Only when children have been carefully taught, learned to discern, enculturated, and mastered skills is it possible for the community to fully trust them and to benefit from their potential (Edelman 1994). Skillful leaders understand this potential and seek out those with promise.

LEARNING TO FEED THE GOOD WOLF

As children grow, they must increasingly satisfy their own needs: material, social, and agentive. This journey to adulthood is often fraught with challenge and difficulties; early learning about which wolf to feed matters. From parents who feel they can handle the job of raising a child, children develop self-efficacy—empowering, affirming, accepting (Bandura 1982, 1986; Dadds and Tully 2019). Children learn to face anger, frustration, brooding, and resentment as they learn to deal with solving problems rationally. They become secure, confident, and self-efficacious as they gradually learn to feed the good wolf with newly acquired skills. These skills are critical in building resilience against countervailing forces of evil that will come into their lives.

Parental Shaping

Ideal parenting is firm but accommodating and open in communication. The child knows her parents have her back (Dadds and Tully 2019). Praising the child for doing what she does well while accepting failures with gracious, kind instructions for improvement teaches the child how to feed the good wolf. This approach enhances self-confidence, self-control, and coping skills, the essential building blocks in managing fear, anger, and blaming (Cattaneo and Chapman 2012). Providing support without teaching ways to cope leaves the child with adequate skills (Dadds and Tully 2019). Then she must struggle for ways to cope without instructions on how to feed the good wolf. Parents are only human—they may either be too directive, destroying the child's ability to learn on her own, or too remote, leaving the child lost. Leaving the child to improvise is often not successful. Essential pieces in the strategy can easily be missed or underemphasized. However, most parents, with love and devotion for their children, do a reasonably good job.

While caring for others does have an innate quality, ways to be caring must be taught (Tomasello 2019). There are cultural rules about ways to care and levels of caring—being nice generally but less nice in dealing with actual threats and enemies. Learning to cope includes discernment about encroachment of the bad wolf and resistance to messages to feed the bad wolf. Learning to feed the good wolf and watching out for the bad wolf are essential life skills learned in childhood. Good parenting leads children toward an adulthood of resilience, self-respect, and caring of others. As adults, children pay it forward: often treating others the way they were treated as children.

Environmental and Epigenetic Influences

Learning to cope may be too narrow a concept for facing environmental and epigenetic influences. Trauma, even generations ago, can affect the brain.

Trauma in the womb and during birth can directly injure brain tissue. One common result of such trauma is reduction in control over violent emotions and actions. The exact location of the trauma matters, but trauma is usually widespread enough to affect at least some relevant brain centers. Fear is focused in the amygdala and aggression more widely in the limbic system. Interpretation of stimuli as frightening and reaction to fear are distributed over the brain, typically following neural pathways from the amygdala and other basal structures to the frontal lobes and the motor centers. Eventually, all the brain is involved. Any trauma can impact the fear-aggression pathways somewhere (Bandura 1982, 1986; Beck 1999).

However, humans are tough. They can adapt to terrible conditions, at least if they have support. Emmy Werner and Ruth Smith (1982, 2001) studied children growing up resilient or emotionally fragile. They found that about 75 percent of children raised in poverty and harsh surroundings in rural Kaua'i in the mid-twentieth century coped well. Half of them had strong, reliable families while 25 percent were redeemed by institutions, such as good schools and churches, the military, and the like. The final 25 percent remained fragile and did not break out of the pattern. They often came from chaotic homes and usually experienced abuse or neglect. Abuse teaches children to abuse, and neglect teaches them to neglect (Agyekumwaa 2016; Wilson 2015).

For children in difficult circumstances, learning to feed the good wolf and learning resilience comes at a cost, including emotional fragility and often physical stresses leading to higher rates of cardiovascular disease and metabolic syndrome proportional to the intensity of the stress (Werner and Smith 1982, 2001). While intervention can help, no one escapes unscathed from a harsh background (Hostinar and Miller 2019; Reynolds et al. 2019).

Learning to feed the good wolf, to face fears, to solve problems without violence, and to discern between good and evil, involves good parenting and guidance from parents and the community. Indeed, it takes a village to raise a child and to teach the child to feed the good wolf.

Learning to Feed the Bad Wolf

Working back from any given violent act is grounding in anger, hatred, or selfish greed. The nexus point is resentment triggered by anything from trivial slights to major disrespect. This is the true "bad wolf": brooding, picking at the sore, ruminating, and reflecting on how unfairly one has been treated by the world. The default solution is to eliminate the cause of the emotional pain. Resentment and brooding feed the bad wolf.

The back story of resentment is both entitlement and weakness. To resent, an individual must feel deprived of some entitlement: respect, food, wealth, control, power, high position. The individual must also feel weak, lacking self-efficacy and the coping skills to fix the situation by ordinary effort, for example, work, negotiation, patience, changing the setting or situation. Resentment is a very dangerous psychic state leading to violent outbreaks, such as mass shooting or genocidal leadership.

A child is very vulnerable to feeding the bad wolf when she feels unsupported in her feelings of fear, weakness, and resentment and has no coping skills to combat these feelings. She is likely to become angry and antagonistic. A young child in such a situation may overcompensate, depending upon immature defenses and failing to learn age-appropriate coping mechanisms. Usually one immature defense mechanism will stick, becoming a stubborn and intractable problem in adulthood. It is most resistant to psychotherapy and life experience and the hardest to bring to full consciousness and self-awareness (Beck 1999; Ellis 1962; Maslow 1970).

Parental Shaping

Harsh, unsupportive parenting is characterized by brutality, abuse, and neglect (Agyekumwaa 2016; Wilson 2015). It teaches the child to feed the bad wolf a toxic diet of abusive behavior. Most parents, however, are not such monsters, but there are other ways to harm the child and teach him to feed the bad wolf. A parent can be harsh and critical, while also, at some level, supportive. Being raised by one highly critical parent and the other parent who retreats in passivity is a common formula for producing a scared, defensive child. Weakness and hypercritical judgment very often go together, either in the same parent or in a couple. This parental pattern teaches fear and fragments the child's developing self-confidence. The child may feel that even the tiniest slight is a total attack on her personhood. Criticizing the child for "imperfect" solutions, and taking over to "fix" the situation, reinforces that she cannot cope. The child learns to fear abandonment and scorn. Frustrated, lacking self-esteem, and angry, the child is locked into narrow walls of insecurity. The bad wolf gets a huge meal.

If parents are strident and highly defensive of their own opinions, condemning everything and everyone who is "different" or the "other," the child is crippled in developing his own views and in learning civil behavior. Raising a child to be caring, to feed the good wolf, includes teaching civility—listening, negotiating, helping, and accepting divergent ways of thinking (Harris 1998). Parents who teach out-of-control fear and hatred channeled into scapegoating teach the child to be a bully, a fearful, brooding child who lacks courage, normative social skills, and self-efficacy. This fragile child has learned to feed the bad wolf.

Environmental and Epigenetic Influences

The capacity to harm, like caring, is innate and can be developed. Imperative is learning the difference between self-defense and protection of loved ones in actual threatening situations versus lashing out in a violent, unpredictable, or gratuitously cruel manner. As discussed above, brain trauma can drive violence through fear-aggression pathways (Bandura 1982, 1986; Beck 1999). Likewise, harsh, fearful, and uncontrollable environments can trigger capacity to harm (Agyekumwaa 2016; Hostinar and Miller 2019; Reynolds et al. 2019; Werner and Smith 1982, 2001).

Facing fears, solving problems without violence, and discerning between good and evil involve guidance from parents and the community. Families and villages sometimes raise children to feed bad wolves. Or, it may be a mix of feeding both wolves. Such fragile children may become fragile adults lacking resilience and efficacy. They are at risk of becoming complicit and conforming to forces of evil that may come into their lives.

SUSCEPTIBILITY TO CONFORMING TO GENOCIDE

Tolerance and openness are a bit of a psychological luxury; they sharply decline when people are fragile, lack efficacy, or they feel their mental energy is exhausted (Tadmor et al. 2018). When control of salient aspects of life is threatened, people tend to blame the "other"—not fate, the economy, the weather, and most certainly not themselves. They tend to see the solution as controlling or eliminating the "other." Fear, resentment, rejection, and harassment are the daily kibble of the bad wolf, especially when such stresses are perceived to have malignant intent (Ames and Fiske 2015). They can become the raw red meat of hatred leading to genocide.

Who is Vulnerable?

Albert Bandura in his book *Moral Disengagement* (2016) points out that participation in harm involves moral disengagement: minimizing, dehumanizing, or justifying. In some circumstances, the culture may condone or actually justify moral disengagement, such as killing in defense of one's self, family, or country (Fiske and Rai 2014; Mueller and Skitka 2020). Under less definitive circumstances, however, ordinary people can also be persuaded to enter into harm, even to the level of genocide. Susceptibility depends upon level of fear, self-efficacy, and genuine worry about status and respect. The "belief in a just world" (Lerner 1980) and cognitive dissonance (Festinger et al. 1956) act as enablers to justify hatred and move toward genocide (Alvarez and

Bachman 2017; Waller 2016). Humans also need to feel in control of their situation (Langer 1983) and will do almost anything to maintain that feeling. Those who are most fragile, lacking strong self-efficacy and moral compass, are more susceptible than others. They lapse into following orders of destruction out of cowardice and hatred. Even the most resilience and morally strong person can succumb with enough pressure. Even the most fearful person can be kept from harming others. Culture provides the pathway and the models.

Alan Fiske and Taj Rai (2014) have argued that almost all violence is moral: it is justified by the moral teachings of the society in question. They point out that violent behavior such as blood revenge, horrific initiation rites, war, raiding, human sacrifice, brutal discipline, and physical punishment have all been considered not only moral but sacred duty in literally thousands of societies around the world. Steven Pinker (2011) reminds us that revenge killings, duels, killing of one's own disobedient children, rape and killing of slaves, and many other forms of mayhem were not only accepted but approved in Western society—including the United States—well into the nineteenth century. Disapproving of such behavior is very recent. Antiwar sentiments are also recent. Taking over land by exterminating its occupants was universal, and broadly accepted, until the mid-nineteenth century.

Fiske and Rai see societies as displaying relational models. These come in four kinds, which can all be combined in one society: "communal sharing: unity . . . authority ranking: hierarchy . . . equality matching: equality [Rawlsian fairness] . . . and market pricing: proportionality" (Fiske and Rai 2014:18–21). There are six "constitutive phases" of moral violence: "creation [of relationships] . . . conduct, enhancement, modulation, and transformation [again of relationships] . . . protection; redress and rectification . . . termination . . . mourning" (sacrifices, self-mutilation, and the like as mourning rituals) (Fiske and Rai 2014:23–24). Violence follows the models: a result of group solidarity (usually against other groups) in unity-driven societies; keeping people in their place in hierarchic ones; maintaining equity in egalitarian societies; and "an eye for an eye, a tooth for a tooth" in market-driven ones. Complex societies can be expected to have all four types of relational models operating inside people's heads and in the cultural spaces, and thus to have violence for all those reasons and more.

Fiske and Rai deal largely with cultural groups and cultural norms. Unusual events like genocide are not quite in the picture, though, for example, Europe's massacres of Jews go back many centuries. Exceptional murder and violence for gain or from psychopathy or sadism are explicitly exempted from their theory, being immoral even to the perpetrators. The problems with this work are numerous. First, and most obvious, there is no explanation of where such morals come from beyond the idea (almost universally agreed) that violence by law enforcers is sometimes necessary to maintain any social order at all. We are left wondering why honor killings, cruel initiation rites, rape, incest, and the like are found in some places and not others.

Second, all societies, and especially all those more complex than a hunting-gathering band, have multiple moral alternatives. One does not have to be a violent barroom brawler in the modern United States, even in the working-class white south (cf. Nisbett and Cohen 1996 on honor and violence in that milieu). Very few Middle Eastern Muslims become terrorists or suicide bombers, despite Western stereotypy. Intimate partner violence is normal in some societies—19 percent of world societies, according to Fiske and Rai (2014:160), a strangely precise figure—but is uncommon and a "marked case" in most. Third, as we have seen, genocide is predicted perfectly by the presence of a leader who takes total power by scapegoating weak groups, and then consolidates and maintains power by killing those groups.

Fourth, Fiske and Rai do not distinguish between genuine cultural rules, individual moral poses, and outrageously lame excuses. Political violence often is clearly due to hatred, however cloaked in rhetoric. Much becomes clear when one listens to playground bullies (the following lines come from our own childhood): "He was littler than me, so I beat him up." "I'm torturing this squirrel to death because it's a varmint, it ain't good for nothin'." "I hit my sister to make her shut up, she was botherin' me." Fiske and Rai quote a number of young peoples' justifications for killing that are no more persuasive. The grown-up forms of such excuses, "all the easy speeches that comfort cruel men" as G. K. Chesterton put it (in the poem "O God of Earth and Altar"), are no less lame for being suave and phrased in proper political language.

The Role of the Evil Leader

Fear can be articulated by leaders and strategies to overcome can be proposed. In his first inaugural address, Franklin Delano Roosevelt said, "The only thing we have to fear is fear itself" (http://historymatters.gmu.edu/d/5057/ %20). He mobilized the nation through the Great Depression and World War II with encouragement to overcome fear. Conversely, the evil leader uses fear as a rallying call and ways to divide and scapegoat. Fearful and resentful adults, well-schooled from childhood on how to feed the bad wolf and facing significant adult challenges, are very susceptible to this message.

The evil leader appears to be strong. He has an uncanny ability to articulate negative-sum gaming, painting the world in steady decline, redeemable only by taking from and eliminating others. He understands that it is easier to rally against a perceived enemy than to unite and build coalitions for a good cause (Bowles 2006; Henrich 2016). He rallies for conformity and exclusionary norms (Henrich 2016). He emanates characteristics of evil authoritarianism.

Table 9.1   Characteristics of the Authoritarian Evil Leader

I'm in power, I'm in charge.
I'm more powerful than you, so I make the rules.
I define the moral and social norms.
Differences are bad, threatening, offensive.
Your job is to obey and follow my dictates.
My first need is to keep you weak and under control through fear.
Any means of control is acceptable including torture and cruelty.

Genocide is moralized as necessary to eliminate hated groups within society. Religion is a particularly easy strategy, since it promotes the values, goals, hopes, and moralities of the culture. Religion may be used to promote not only hatred but also nationalism and militarism. Those fearful and fragile faithful potentially can be turned into fanatic haters and mindless followers, even if their religion teaches love and tolerance. Genocide is predicted perfectly by evil leaders who use religion or ideology to assume moral power and spin a message of hatred for others who do not fit the paradigm. Historically and currently there are many examples of this axiom. They include some fundamentalist branches of Christianity and Islam, Marxist socialism, and military dictatorships. Hitler promoted genocide, the "final solution," as necessary to save the German people from degenerate enemies—Jews, Roma, homosexuals, and other hated groups. Some historians have proposed that Hitler actually believed such groups are utterly degenerate and saw himself as a savior. The record does not substantiate that position. He fought his way to power by underhanded and cowardly murder, blackmail, double-dealing, targeting any group unpopular at the time, and other morally dubious means (Rosenbaum 2014). How much the Germans believed their own traditional, generally hateful stereotypes of Jews is also controversial. Were they "willing executioners," as Daniel Goldhagen (1996) held, or less credulous (Newman 2002)? Hitler fed upon the fears and vulnerabilities of the most angry and fragile Germans.

Some, like Oskar Schindler, resisted. Evil leaders, like Hitler, are not devoted saviors but manipulators, despising and controlling vulnerable followers (Dikötter 2019; Rummel 1998). The break point in complicity and conformity is when the evil leader grabs enough power and social visibility in a challenging period to exploit weak defensiveness and flip the population into widespread expression of hatred and eventually genocide. Rwanda provides a particularly well-studied example (Nyseth Brehm 2017a, 2017b).

As John Pavlovitz (2020) asserts:

The metamorphosis of a people begins with an opportunistic leader who understands the power of weaponized fear, who feeds them a steady diet of the things that terrify them: misinformation, fake emergencies, and abject lies all designed to create an urgency in them and to make them feel hopelessly assailed. (https://johnpavlovitz.com/2019/08/30/this-is-how-holocausts-happen/?fbclid=IwAR 12OdlpIuJY_Iyw3cfVfk-Vrbao9Yn-kT8_ER1-otnk2dS7VwXDLQ_3zVw)

RESPONSE AND REMORSE AFTER GENOCIDE

After a genocide is over, most complicit people say that they conformed out of fear. They are usually unwilling to admit anything further, although some have written about their remorse. Some never relent, such as Ezra Pound and Martin Heidegger (Bourdieu 1991 per Heidegger's allegiance to fascism). Even today, there are loyal Maoists in China and some Americans who voice the opinion that genocide committed against Native Americans was moral because they were underutilizing productive resources (Newman 2020, passim).

SUMMARY

Rare are those persons, like Viktor Frankl and Oskar Schindler, who have the moral stamina and self-efficacy to resist the march of genocide (Anderton and Brauer 2019). Our best hope to avert the moral weakness of complicity is to show children how to feed the good wolf, guiding their moral compass, and providing opportunities to develop coping skills and self-efficacy.

Evil is almost always due to power challenged. Rulers consolidating dictatorship, totalitarian rulers under threat, schoolyard bullies dominating weak but smart kids, insecure and inadequate husbands beating wives, politicians facing trial, oil company bosses facing better energy generation and consequent loss of power and position, drug lords facing upstart thugs all have this in common, and above all majorities facing imagined challenge by immigrants and minorities. The bad wolf is fed by fear socially channeled into scapegoating and bullying, by culture and society based on top-down power that is poorly restrained, and by personal grievance and offense coming out in hate and irrational harm. This may be deployed in the service of greed, sadism, defense, or "honor," but the basic animal is the same. The good wolf is fed by the opposite: dealing with problems as rationally and peacefully as possible, in a society where equality and tolerance are values. This too may be deployed for gain or defense or any other purpose. As long as humans are social animals with strong fight-flight-freeze responses, the chain from defense to hostility to evil is sure to be reinvented, and to become popular wherever displaced aggression is socially tolerated. As long as human childrearing is imperfect, leading to weak but resentful children and adults, evil leaders will take advantage of that weakness and resentment.

Evil is not inevitable, and can be prevented, but it takes over when given even a small chance, due to the human fight responses to threat and stress. Almost any person will become evil if pressured enough, but almost any person can be kept from evil if pressured in that direction. Culture usually provides both good and bad models and teachings. In the next and final chapter, we will look at some ways to build a stronger, less hateful world, one that can recognize the early signs of genocide formation, and intervene with messages and strategies of hope and peace.

Chapter 10

The Food of the Good Wolf

"In time we hate that which we often fear"

William Shakespeare (*Antony and Cleopatra* Act I, scene 3)

SUMMARY OF OUR MODEL

The whole progress of evil consists of four steps, at each of which an intervention is necessary to stop evil from occurring. First is the endless worry, anxiety, and threat to personal standing that dominate life. This must be combated by assuring security of physical needs and then using the Serenity Prayer or an equivalent: courage, patience, and wisdom. Second is the scared and defensive anger and rage that result from challenge; these are inevitably disproportionate to the cause, since they come out of the daily anxiety and worry as well as the slight itself. This escalation must be met by de-escalation: talking people down, calming the situation, finding reasonable solutions. Third is projection, displacement, and scapegoating—in other words, hatred and bigotry—which must be directly fought by every means possible, from explaining the truth to actual restraint of behavior. Fourth is outright violence against scapegoated groups, which of course must be stopped by force. At all stages, it is not enough to stop bad behavior; it must be replaced by good behavior—rational coping, proactive help, proactive tolerance, and mutual aid.

THE PROBLEM OF HATRED

Hate is our worst problem. It is the outpouring of fear and cowardice. We need to make it unacceptable through a moral and social order that keeps the good wolf well fed and the bad one starved (Anderson 2010). The first rule of morality, per Kant, is to accept all people, and ultimately all beings, as having a valid claim to quality of life: people are ends, not means; subjects, not objects (Kant 2002 [1785]). The Japanese have a closely similar concept, *ikigai*, "life value," and the Chinese *ren*, "humaneness," is similar.

Our survival on this planet depends upon which wolf we feed. The good wolf thrives on empathy, compassion, respect, mutual aid, and tolerance. The bad wolf grows fat on fear and hatred, manifested as terror, rage, violence, and sometimes genocide. The purpose of this book is to look at why individuals and even whole nations, against all rational best interests, conform and comply with the cascade that leads to genocide.

Specific social actions can fight hatred. We feel that only by uniting economic incentives, charismatic leadership, and common morality will hatred be confronted. We need positive, inclusive, and factual dialogue. This includes *damping down conflicts* caused by desire for wealth, power, and approval; *balancing power* so that it is distributed equally before the law with checks and balances; a wide network of *search for truth*—science in a broad sense—instead of religious or ideological claims for absolute truth or nihilistic denial of truth's existence. We need *integrity*, never humanity's strong point. It has eroded due to loss of community, the rise of giant corporations, passivity-creating media, and tolerance of lying. Failure to keep commitments is modeled all too well and often by political leaders. Such actions require retributive and restorative justice (Li and Leidner 2020).

We need ways of healing and rejuvenation, such as mindful meditation to reduce fear, defensiveness, and intolerance (Park and Pyszczynski 2019). We also need strong advocacy. As an example of excellent advocacy, the Southern Poverty Law Center leads in identifying measurable actions to fight hatred:

- Act
- Join forces
- Support victims
- Speak up
- Educate yourself
- Create alternatives
- Pressure leaders
- Stay engaged
- Teach acceptance
- Dig deeper

(see https://www.splcenter.org/20170814/ten-ways-fight-hate-community-response-guide).

The reason that feeding the good wolf so often fails is not mere selfishness. It is complicity with hatred and unwillingness to cooperate with or value others. To survive and thrive, we need to work with others as equals—learning, changing, and growing. On this journey, we are all in this together.

THE FOOD OF THE GOOD WOLF

There are powerful actions that create social change—*education*, *governance*, and *ecology* conveyed through *messages* that build and support a strong society.

Education That Empowers

We desperately need an educational system that creates and fosters self-confidence; critical, independent thinking; and concern for quality of life. Teaching students *how to learn*, discerning quantifiable truth and accuracy from falsehood, and how to search out knowledge is most important for educated citizens. These skills are the necessary building blocks to resisting defensiveness, hatred, and mindless conformity.

Science

Science education must teach verified science, not held hostage to falsehood and propaganda. The Trump administration, including many Republicans in Congress, have launched a full-scale war against science (2020; see also Michaels 2008; Oreskes and Conway 2010). They do not stop with dismissing science that is embarrassing to their corporate donors or counter to their political positions. The concept of truth is a casualty to "alternative facts" and political agendas that negate the scientific method of proof, evidence, and data as equal to unsubstantiated and potentially dangerous opinions. Examples include denial of climate change, claims that tobacco and pesticides are harmless to humans, racism under the guise of human qualities based upon "race," quack treatments for illness, and unfounded antivaccination statements. Freedom of speech does not extend to the freedom to teach lies. This is among the most immediate and critical of education needs.

Civics

Education needs to return to focus on civics, basic civil morality, and the responsibilities of citizenship. American history based upon the ideals that founded the nation and examples of progress over time need to be taught without denying the jingoistic idolization of the nation or the brutality of past and continuing social ills, such as slavery, genocide, and ongoing racism. Educators have the capacity to be very powerful in modeling civil behavior, inclusion, and commitment to social justice.

Social and Ethical Behavior

Civil behavior and conflict resolution are critical to dealing with fear and anger, and learning cooperative behavior, all necessary for productive citizenship. Part of education is discussion of the realities of failure to deal with fear and anger—domestic violence, bullying, genocide, and war. Feeding the bad wolf by denying fears, brooding, resentment, anger escalation, and hatred needs to be discussed with focus on solution. The cascade of fear, hatred, and violence and the profile of the bully, from the school yard to the nation and the world, are critical pieces to an education grounded in civility and social justice. Exemplars of social justice and civility enforced by governance as well as dissection and analysis of failures can be taught to students of all ages, from the tiny preschool child to the graduate student.

Skills

Across the world, traditional education has always taught skills through apprenticeship learning and active participation. It has conveyed cultural values and abstract principles through stories, songs, and religion (Anderson 2011; Kopnina and Shoreman-Ouimet 2011). The story of which wolf to feed is a classic example of teaching a cultural value. However, such ordinary declarative knowledge is no longer adequate. Knowledge is no longer local. Privatization, standardized tests, isolated religious instruction, and poor funding are seriously impacting the public school system and the education of youth (Ravitch 2010, 2014, 2020). Increasingly education has focused on drilling students to pass standardized tests rather than enabling critical thinking and creativity. Some students even report writing stories and poems and solving problems surreptitiously because they have been discouraged from such activities (ENA, personal experience). Teaching students how to learn, how to resist mindless complicity, and how to contribute to a cooperative, tolerant world is one of the most powerful ways to avoid hatred and conformity to genocide.

Governance That Protects

The first responsibility of government is generally understood to be protection of citizens. Historically, that was defined as military protection, with economic protection added in the twentieth century. Today, there are serious dangers facing citizens—climate change, environmental pollution, violent politics, and risks to the health of the public. Governance that protects assumes responsibility for environmental and public health protection, security from hate crimes, legal defense of economic livelihood, and safe keeping of national historic and natural treasures.

Government and Genocide

Historically, genocide has arisen in every form of governance except true democracy characterized by equality and equal rights before the law. It has occurred in governments defining themselves as socialist, capitalist, autocratic, and monarchic (Anderson and Anderson 2013). Even true democracy faces ongoing challenges of violence, crime, and war, but, by definition, has legal and economic protections against the development of genocide. Economic deprivation creates conditions of fear and hatred encouraging exclusionary ideologies. Likewise, giant primary-production interests that fund and organize dissension against the economic wellbeing of the populace are culpable in promoting the conditions leading to genocide. To prevent genocide, the legal system and laws must exist within a moral shell that promotes equity and justice. Fair and equitable governance creates conditions that reduce fear and threat, empower individual capability to deal with threat, promote civility and inclusion, and reduce to hatred and harm toward the "other."

Transparency and Justice in Governance

We need to limit dark money and big money in politics. This starts with a Constitutional amendment making all political money fully transparent and prohibiting politicians from seeking self-aggrandizing economic interest in campaign funding. We need to ban subsidies as much as possible, and *certainly* ban subsidies to maintain dinosaur industries that cost more than they produce (Harvey et al. 2019; see also Coady et al. 2017; Ellsmoor 2019; Kirby 2017; Van Lierop 2019). We must block the chain from lobbyist to "regulator." Those who lobby for industry that damages the environment and erodes public health must not simultaneously be the government regulator. Government needs to account for the profitability and actual social, environmental, and financial costs of damaging industries. Oil is profitable only because its real costs are passed on as externalities (Anderson 2010; cf. Metcalf 2020). A transparent government, protecting the citizens needs to eliminate giant primary-production interests, breaking statal, parastatal, and private corporations into small, accountable entities. It also involves engaging in major economic repair of devastated urban and rural communities in the United States.

Civil Rights and Equity

We need an entire new civil rights movement, focused immediately on putting an end to partisan purging of voter rolls, gerrymandering, and new Jim Crow laws. Progress comes from outlawing the bad and enforcing minimal civil decency, relative economic freedom within moral limits, as Adam Smith argued, and promoting equity in development of knowledge and skills.

Freedom of speech must be defended, but does not include direct incitement to violence or hate crimes, libel, or false advertising especially on the part of governing officials. Campaign lies, skewed media presentations, and language advocating rabid hatred lead to violence. The right to racist rhetoric stops when it impinges on others. Promoting civility and fighting racist, religious, and ideological bigotry needs to be modeled by governance that calls for tolerance, valuing diversity, and national solidarity. Promoting the right to civil, nonviolent resistance is a way that governance protects and works well, as exemplified by Gandhi's leadership in India and the civil rights movement in the United States (Chenoweth and Stephan 2012). Proposals to make campaign speeches follow the laws for sworn testimony need to be considered seriously.

Adam Smith (1910 [1776]) described government, economics, and ethics as existing in a moral shell. For the twenty-first century, that shell needs to be inclusive, protecting individuals and groups who are not dispensable, worthless, or deserving of extermination by reason of religion, social class, or ethnicity. The only way for governance to truly protect is to allow peaceful expression and demonstrations of differences, media campaigns dedicated to promoting inclusion and encouraging protective legislation, and opportunities for citizens to be involved in governance and voted into office at all levels (Chenowith and Stephan 2012). These are the measures that have worked for protection of workers, civil rights, antiwar and environmental movements, and every other popular cause that got beyond shouting and legislated into the law of the land. Absolutely necessary is the right to recourse. People who are injured must be able to sue, to protest, to speak out, to vote evil leaders out, and to defend themselves in any reasonable way.

Ecology That Sustains

Genocide need not be outright murder. Today, levels of global warming and pollution are leading to thousands of excess deaths, and this will become millions in the near future unless we act. Callousness, structural violence, and bureaupathy are as deadly as guns. We need to think of ecology in terms of respect and sustainability. With a proper spirit of respect, we will be able to preserve species and environments and to avoid destruction by pollutants and excessive construction. In the short run, we have to fall back on laws that support this respect. The framework existing as of 2016 was inadequate, but it was a good start. Now it is lost, and we will have to start over, hopefully with better laws to be designed in future. We need to draw on the wisdom of those traditional moralities teaching respect for all beings. Children absorb this wisdom at a very young age. They grow up remembering that trees, fish, habitats, and all species need to be regarded as worthy of consideration, used sustainably, and protected for future generations (Louv 2019). Much of the Western world has been an outlier to this traditional prudence, engaging in adversarial fashion toward and destroying natural resources.

Balancing environmental protection against immediate use is always difficult and requires much more attention. Long-term, wide-flung interests should prevail above short-term, narrow ones. However, short-term needs must be considered, because failure to attend to immediate threats and concerns can kill before the long term is reached. For example, as of April 2020, in an effort to limit contagion during the Covid-19 pandemic, California relaxed its environmental protection law that shoppers should supply their own shopping bags; for safety, shoppers were required to use merchant-supplied plastic bags instead of providing personal bags when purchasing household supplies. (See https://www.nytimes.com/2020/04/24/us/california -plastic-bag-ban-coronavirus.html.)

These concerns are a tension in balancing human needs and environmental damage, especially species extinction. Once extinct, a species cannot be brought back. Many protected species are obviously economically and ecologically valuable. With others, with currently limited knowledge, we have no idea of how they fit into the natural scheme. Yet, but we have witnessed how loss of a single species can cause meltdown of a whole ecological system. We need bats for fruit pollination and bees for honey. A new pesticide, an epidemic, a rampantly multiplying introduced pest, or an ill-considered human action can rapidly change a species from common to endangered. The Endangered Species Act has been under permanent attack by Republicans since it was proposed. The ostensible reason is that the act saves worthless weeds and bugs at the expense of human interests. The real reason is that it freezes up habitat that corporate interests want to use (Turner and Isenberg 2018).

Priority Sustainability Areas

Certain species are at critical points of endangerment and some sectors of the environment are under great threat. These are areas that need immediate attention in order to maintain environmental sustainability (see Table 10.1).

While the Endangered Species Act has had significant influence on *biodiversity and endangered species preservation*, some areas of concern remain.

Table 10.1   Priority Environmental Sustainability Concerns

Biodiversity and endangered species preservation
Pollution
Land management
Agricultural and fishing practices
Quality of urban life
Green spaces, recreation areas and national monuments

One is the continued trade in endangered species, often to businesses and individuals wanting "exotic" animals and plants. Another is trophy hunting. While most of safari adventures these days involve shooting only with a camera, there still are those who hunt endangered animals to the point of extinction, such as the "big game" hunting by Eric Trump and Donald Trump Jr.

There is no question that the world is warming rapidly, and that greenhouse gases are the main reason. The fossil fuel industry is responsible for most pollution resulting in global warming. The outright denialist positions are now apparently monopolized by public relations people working for fossil fuel corporations. Some denialists point to historical cycles of global warming such as the massive outpouring of carbon dioxide from volcanoes, about 50 million years ago. The Eocene world warmed rapidly and dramatically, stayed warm for about 200,000 years, and then cooled so fast that trees growing in the high Arctic froze in place. Much later Arctic explorers used some of these trees for firewood, later discovering that their firewood was 50 million years old!

Globally today, greenhouse gases, comparable to those released by the volcanoes, are caused by human consumption. Most is from poorly regulated transportation-linked carbon dioxide emission as well as methane gas from animal wastes as human demand for meat products increase. Rising sea levels and rising thermal temperature are resulting in dangerous human environs, such as the lowland Middle East where soaring temperatures already threaten human survival (Xu et al. 2020). U.S. federal government attempts to override state laws on air and water pollution as well as failure to respond to water crisis situations, as witnessed in Detroit, put large segments of the population, especially those most vulnerable, at risk. The U.S. abdication of the Paris Accords sends a strong message to a world struggling with global warming and hazardous climate changes.

Land management is a critical issue. For instance, forestry has also suffered from a see-saw battle between lockdown preservation and totally destructive and wasteful clear-cutting. Wiser solutions (reforestation, controlled burning, thinning) have been well known for over 100 years but are rarely invoked today. Personal research from satellite photographs and ground truthing in Oregon is instructive: one finds tiny pockets of overcrowded locked-down preserves, surrounded by vast moonscapes of badly recovering clear-cut land (ENA 1962–2020). Oregon has lost most of its songbirds, as well as its forestry futures. Grasslands, wetlands and streams, brushlands, and deserts are, likewise, at risk. Globally, there is a desperate need to preserve and maintain wilderness areas to offset the effect of damaging greenhouse gases.

Coupled with land management are unsustainable *agricultural and fishing practices*. Pesticides and deadly chemicals poison our food, much of which goes to waste from poor food management preservation at corporate and household levels. Much of prime agriculture land is sacrificed to urbanization and production of ecocidal plants toxic to human health, like palm oil. Within the last two centuries, California has urbanized almost a third of its farmland, some of the best in the world. Within our living memories, the San Jose Valley, now Silicon Valley, was among the most productive orchard land in the world. Now there are barely any orchards. Fish is a sustainable and highly nutritious food. At the current global rates of overfishing, stripping the seas of its wealth, it is predicted that there will be no wild commercial fisheries by 2050 (Kroodsma et al. 2018; Worm et al. 2006).

The built environment, the great urban centers, are where 55 percent of the world's population, four billion people, live. This is projected to increase to six billion by the year 2045. (See www.worldbank.org/en/topic/urbandev elopment.) The *quality of urban life*, in the United States as well as across the world, is often a dismal environment, sprawling, crowded blight. While a few model cities have excellent facilities, transportation, green spaces, and access to education and the arts, most struggle with poverty, crime, and social injustice. (See https://www.urban.org/sites/default/files/publication/89491/ 2017.04.03_urban_blight_and_public_health_vprn_report_finalized.pdf.)

Green spaces, recreation areas, and national monuments, places of peace, a reflection of the soul of the nation, are under siege in many places. National treasures, like the great national and state parks in the United States, are an example. Preserving the ancient redwood trees in northern California has been an ongoing battle, mostly led by concerned citizens. (See https://www .savetheredwoods.org/redwoods.) One failure in the enthusiasm to develop new national monuments and public lands has been lack of due process with local populations. While land protection is critical, so is local input for both for pragmatic and democratic reasons.

Implementing "Social Tipping Interventions"

We need mechanisms for moving quickly for restorative action. Ilona Otto and colleagues (2020) point out that social tipping interventions could make the world move away from fossil fuels fast enough to save the planet and its billions of humans and other species from collapse. "These social tipping interventions comprise removing fossil fuel subsidies and incentivizing decentralized energy generation, building carbon-neutral cities, divesting from assets linked to fossil fuels, revealing the moral implications of fossil fuels, strengthening climate education and engagement, and disclosing greenhouse gas emissions information" (Otto et al. 2020:2354).

It is not as difficult as most people think if political landmines can be avoided. Paul Hawken, editor of the book *Drawdown* (2017), identifies 100 relatively manageable ways, ranked from most to least effective, to reduce carbon in the atmosphere, slow down global climate change, and move toward an ecology that sustains. First, in an increasing hot world, is using state-of-the-art refrigeration and air conditioning technology which could enormously reduce carbon footprint. Next is using wind energy in place of fossil fuels. Ultimately, the solution must extend to clean power which is a political fight. Saving the environment from sunsetting interests such as Big Oil and Big Agribusiness means switching to renewable wind and sun energy.

The ideal economic adjustment is one in which destructive activities are penalized rather than subsidized. It is one in which conservation and sustainable management are valued instead of discounted. Such a model existed in old Southeast Asia. Nobody then assessed economic growth, though the governments did tax value created. What mattered was saving forests and fruit trees, growing rich and complex crop assemblages, creating beautiful arts, living happily, and letting others live as they wished. Societies were ruled by kings, but were astonishingly free and open. The landscapes were beautiful, and got richer, lusher, and more diverse over time, because agriculture was devoted to producing human food rather than industrial goods. There was war and killing, but nothing remotely like what we have seen in the past 100 years in the world. The one great problem was disease, which was rampant, but with modern medicine this has been stopped, and lifespans are comparable to and exceed those in the West. The problems now are rapid population growth in a context of even more rapid shift to Western industrialization. Similar, cultures less materially successful, such as the Maya of Mexico and Central America, have been notably good at maintaining ecosystems.

A particularly compelling point from Hawken's book, in line with the World Health Organization Sustainable Development Goals, is the recommendation for universal education for girls. Better educated girls become adult women who contribute to the national economy, participate more fully in nation building, are generally healthier, and have smaller families. (See https://www.unicef.org/education/girls-education.) Hawken allows that this checklist of 100 interventions would not be sufficient in themselves but are concrete, doable actions at global, national, and household levels. With widespread implementation, they would probably be sufficient to improve human health and potential and reverse greenhouse gas increases and other major environmental stresses while costing a fraction compared to doing nothing. The total estimated cost would be less, in today's economy, than the cost of mobilization in World War II. It would dampen down the trillions of dollars spent subsidizing, fossil fuel extraction, a form of production that could not exist without heavy government financing.

Land management is a way to blot up 20 percent of atmospheric carbon, especially preserving and restoring forests. Reforestation, silvo-pasture (savanna grazing, with livestock and tree-cropping together), wetland protection, mangrove and tropical forest conservation, and perennial grass restoration are all highly effective. Agricultural practices such as planting nitrogen-fixing grains, perennial grain crops and other perennials; mosaic tree cropping; targeted fertilizing and pest control; producing less meat; growing bamboo and hemp in place of plastics for a vast range of industrial purposes; and decreasing food waste would eliminate most of the 10 percent of greenhouse gases produced by industrial agriculture (Hawken et al. 2017).

In the *Proceedings of the National Academy of Sciences*, Griscom et al. (2017) show that intensive bio-farming would also greatly reduce carbon footprint. This is an area when the individual can make a difference. Shaded coffee plantations are wildlife havens, not only for native wildlife but also for migratory birds while sun-drenched plantations are biological deserts. Whole bird species in Latin America depend on shade-grown plantations and in turn, they eat the mosquitoes that carry malaria, dengue and Zika virus. A single coffee drinker of shade-grown coffee can maintain both a significant coffee patch and bird population. Another place where an individual can make a difference is in home landscaping. Creating an oasis of plants native to the area can have an effect far beyond the property line.

Planting fruit trees using only organic pest control and fertilizer protects the environment as well as food security. Some cities have developed varying degrees of edible landscaping. Tashkent, Uzbekistan, where ENA did research on Central Asian foodways in 2019, was destroyed by a 5.1 Richter earthquake in 1966. It subsequently redeveloped the city as a garden city with fruit trees as much of the urban landscaping. Mulberries stain the streets dramatically in late spring, but no one complains—they are too busy eating the mulberries, which are devoured as high as the tallest person or most agile climber can reach. (See https://reliefweb.int/report/uzbekistan/1966-2016-50 -years-tashkent-earthquake.) While none of this will "save the world," every small act, including eating less meat and more vegetarian cuisine, can be thought of protecting the earth from a few minutes of biodeterioration.

Many critics have attacked Hawken's work, insisting that individual acts are too minor to matter. Apparently, they think that unless the revolution is at hand, we might as well go on polluting and destroying. Obviously, massive global action is needed but, in the meantime, there are countless small things that help, including political action and supporting candidates that support a sustainable environment. As discussed under *Education to Empower*, educating our children to understand the science of ecology and to love and protect the natural world are the most important.

Messages to Build and Support a Strong Society

Social and cultural evolution to deal with fear, hatred, and the sequelae of violence require individual and systemic support and change. The oft-heard argument that changing oneself is a waste of time as only vast social intervention matters is a self-defeating perspective. Without acknowledging the need for and working toward changing ourselves, will we ever have the courage to correct systemic processes. Individuals working within existing structures can often have substantial influence on modifying and correcting systems. As anthropologist Margaret Mead so wisely stated, "Never doubt that a small group of thoughtful, committed citizens can change the world; indeed, it's the only thing that ever has." (See https://www.goalcast.com/2018/04/09/11 -margaret-mead-quotes.) Individual and system changes affecting education, governance, and the ecology are imparted through the conduit of social messages. Well delivered, these messages need to address the *purpose* of society, means of *solving problems and conflicts*, ways to provide *mutual support and empathy*, and *space for expression of spirituality*.

Purpose

Viktor Frankl observed that survivors of Hitler's concentration camps had something deeply important for which to live. Usually, this was family, a calling, or spiritual expression. He extended his findings over his lifetime, learning that most people, not just concentration camp survivors, desire to have deep meaning in their lives (Frankl 1959, 1978, 2019). Nothing is more meaningful than fighting for a cause, especially one that addresses safety, wellbeing, or opposing evil, such as hatred, lies, oppression, cruelty, or abuse of power. Obstructing such evil, however, often involves fighting against real enemies. Addressing evil directly and explicitly may result in conflicts, but engaging in such clashes can be one of the most powerful ways to give meaning to life (Anderson 1995; Rovenpor et al. 2019). Before escalation of conflict, even for righteous causes, the first lines of action are rational discourse, enforcement of laws, calls to compassion, and dampening down destructive anger (Batson 2011; Beck 1999; Maslow 1970; McLaren 2013; Zaki 2019).

Rational Means of Problem Solving and Conflict Resolution

Messages that build self-efficacy, independent thinking, and skills in conflict resolution are critical to abating fear and complicity in the face of conflict.

There are times when acquiescence is wrong and "peace" is not the best solution. The Quaker and abolitionist response to slavery was an example. Involvement in this movement is part of the rich legacy of BA's family. Rational discourse and nonviolent opposition were the first approaches, even when the law did not support the moral premise of enslavement. As David Hume said, "Reason is, and must ever be, the slave of the passions" (Hume 1969 [1739–1740]:462). It matters to get the passions right, such that reason is the slave of the better ones.

As espoused by the Founding Fathers in the U.S. Constitution, the basic principle of life, liberty, and the pursuit of happiness implies equity, an issue with which the United States has struggled historically. There are limits to freedom, enslavement of another person or the right to bully others is not a right. Thus, is the need for conflict-resolution mechanisms (Beals and Siegal 1966) educating on ways to address conflict without escalation. Messages include support of civil rights and inclusion of scientifically correct information. They call for social responsibility, as described by Adam Smith (1910 [1776]) in his discussion of management of free, small-scale competition. Messages that build a strong society encourage humans to strive for a high level of civil behavior and honesty.

Very few ways of feeding the good wolf have worked in the past, but those few have worked very well. Given the human condition, they largely add up to empowerment of individuals through provision of human rights. We also need to go back to civility in society, as long argued by Jurgen Habermas (1987), and stop fighting each other over every change. By far the best way has been guaranteeing civil and human rights, equal for all, before the law, and enforced strictly by executive and court action. This has eroded disastrously in the United States, but grown steadily in much of Western Europe.

Gandhi, Martin Luther King Jr., and Nelson Mandela exemplify the most important: appealing to solidarity and natural human social goodness in the face of oppression. Next most important and effective has been empowerment. Doing scientific research to find out what improves the human condition is a strong third. Forthrightly opposing evil is a long fourth, but still needs to be done.

Group hatred has traditionally been addressed by getting the groups together in positive situations, giving them common goals or working with the common purposes they already have, affirming irenic and tolerant values, stressing the advantages of diversity, looking for common ground, striving to make groups as equal as possible, defending civil rights and explaining why those are beneficial to all. Some traditional societies have dealt with potential religious conflicts for centuries, and managed them by a number of social rules and strategies. The people of Gondar, an Ethiopian city that is a traditional stronghold of Christianity but has a large Muslim population, have learned to get along, and have taken ISIS in stride, partly by casting it as non-Muslim or otherwise aberrant (Dulin 2017). Similar accommodations have worked until recently in many countries, but the breakdown of very old and long-established ones in Iraq, Syria, and China bodes ill for the future.

The standard methods of increasing happiness—gratitude, good thoughts, reaffirming values, and mindfulness (Lyubomirsky 2007)—are also of some use, but never transformed a society. Only uniting economic incentives, charismatic leaders, and common morality ever works to improve conditions. We need positive, inclusive, and rational dialogue that is factual and hopeful. We need healing and rejuvenation. Recall, also, that mindful meditation reduces existential fear and thus defensiveness and intolerance (Park and Pyszczynski 2019). The reason that advancing the good so often fails is not mere selfishness. It is antagonism to cooperating and to working with others as equals, especially as seen in refusal to learn, change, and self-improve as part of the process. The cure is rational dialogue and valuing conflict resolution. We are all in this struggle together.

Providing Mutual Support and Empathy

The main pillars of mutual aid and empathy are caring, charity, and peace. These inspire us toward compassion expressed in solidarity and mutual aid. We feed the hungry, heal the sick, and care for the vulnerable (see Romans 12:6). Helping requires confidence and courage, hence the importance of raising children with progressively more rights and responsibilities. Jamil Zaki, in *The War for Kindness* (2019), points out that dealing with real-world problems involves empathy: reforming criminals, teaching police to be community servants rather than "warriors," teaching autistic children, and simply helping ordinary people with problems. People have different strengths and skills, allowing for mutual aid and empathy in complex societies and most people want to help others and do right by them.

From a general sense of "we're all in this together," the first personal virtues are openness, warmth, interest in the world, self-confidence, and ability to enjoy life. These were highlighted by Aristotle (1953), but they have been amazingly neglected since his fourth-century-BCE days. These imply a set of learned personal orientations: caring, compassion, civility, considerateness, reasonableness, respect, and—perhaps above all—responsibility. These, especially responsibility, drive the values that create peace and unity in society: solidarity, tolerance, valuing diversity, mutual aid, and empowerment; thus, for society, peace, justice, fairness, equality, truth, and inquiry (as argued by Rawls 1971).

Empathy and altruism are linked; psychological studies have unpacked both. Humans are wired for empathy in ways unknown among other animals. We can build on that by learning to be much more empathetic than is "natural" from the genetic base. We are experts at putting ourselves in others' places, feeling what they feel, and understanding how they could react to situations. Daniel Batson (2011), a leading expert on empathy, points out that these are different things. Understanding others' feelings, matching those feelings, and understanding how our own feelings can be different from others are all different agendas. Lack of empathy is, of course, far too typical of bureaucrats and governments, and of many ordinary people who have either never learned real empathy or have suppressed what they know (Baron-Cohen 2011). Batson shows that altruism goes beyond this: we need to value others. We have seen that understanding the feelings of others can make cruelty worse; the sadist can use understanding and sensitivity to devise the most fiendish tortures. This is well known from the annals of both crime and Hitler's death camps (Baumeister 1997).

Batson further points out that empathy and altruism are not enough. They can make people unfair. One naturally has more empathy to one's family and friends than to strangers, and thus tends to skew altruism. The extreme is reached in those superrich families that take care of their own very well indeed while giving nothing to charity. Batson, a Kantian who follows Kant and Rawls into a realm of absolute ethics of fairness and principle, opposes such narrow empathy to his general principles of fairness. However, in a particularly thoughtful passage (Batson 2011:220–224), he traces the limits of extreme fairness: not only can we not really do it—family ties are generally too strong—but we are also masters at rationalizing, excusing, justifying, and otherwise weaseling out of our principles, when emotions are strong. One may add that with my limited resources we can benefit our family a great deal, but can do virtually nothing for the masses of India; if we divided our wealth equally among them, none would get even one-thousandth of a cent.

Social messages promoting mutual aid and empathy are complex. Wayne Te Brake (2017), in his historical studies, describes how nation-states have had to deliberatively facilitate the process of harmony and mutual aid, although most people in close proximity have no choice but to get along. Studies show that humans are good at both cheating on mutuality and on detecting cheaters and they use strong measures to stop them, for example, shaming, ostracism, and physical punishment (Tomasello 2016; Wrangham 2019). The only problem is that individual messages, especially punitive ones, are not sufficient. Broad social messages of sustained mutuality and development of empathy for the "other" are needed to nurture the innate moral sense of mutual aid and generosity that seem inherent in humans.

We must make moral choices, not simply economic ones. We must make moral choices to help people rather than hurt them. That involves honesty with ourselves about the ways that weakness, resentment, overreaction to trivial or imagined slights, and overreaction to trivial harms combine to feed the bad wolf and thus feed displacing resentment onto weaker people and onto the natural world. Then we must work to feed the good wolf across the world. The food of the good wolf is caring and consideration for all, empowering others through decent, supportive, respectful behavior.

Space for Spiritual Expression

Throughout history, humans have had to cope with existential questions of good and evil. As Durkheim (1912) noted, religion is the collective representation of the community, the way that a community projects its image on the universe. The spiritual world, in turn, represents the human world, not exactly as the people of the community really are, but as they wish to be. As such, the spiritual world has messages for teaching morality to the community and in every religion, there are countless saints, sages, holy men and women, and teachers who have translated these messages.

Since any human community is a diverse mix of good and bad, religions are inevitably a mixture of high ethics and low venality and hatred, notoriously the excuse for many of the most horrific mass murders and genocides. Even the noblest get tarnished. Degree of intolerance for heresies, including the most minor and trivial, tracks religion turned evil, the opposite of ecumenism or tolerance. The common theme of religion turned evil is obsession with hierarchy and control, especially over vulnerable members of society. It was in this context that Lord Acton coined his famous line in 1887: "Power tends to corrupt, and absolute power corrupts absolutely." (See https://www.acton.org/research/lord-acton-quote-archive.) (And it is worth repeating here Rudolph Rummel's corollary, "Power kills, and absolute Power kills absolutely"; Rummel 1994:1.)

In the modern world, belief in classic religions is waning. The collapse of small-scale, intimate communities and the rise of vast, amorphous agglomerations have left many people feeling that uncontrollable, impersonal forces rule their lives. Some argue that religion is "the problem," and that religion is "dead," but the alternatives do not have a good track record. Nationalism, fascism, capitalism, and communism are leading alternative ideologies, and they have demonstrated limited ability to satisfy the need for the divine or to guide morals. All the great religions of the world and spiritual teachings speak to striving for morality and honoring all creatures as fellow travelers on the earth. Space for spirituality in messages is essential and denying this space is a recipe for fear, exclusion, "othering," and even genocide.

SUMMARY

The good wolf thrives on empathy, compassion, respect, mutual aid, and tolerance. The bad wolf grows fat on fear and hatred. The purpose of this book is to look at why, against all rational best interests, individuals and even whole nations, feed the bad wolf—conforming with the cascade of genocide. We also explore ways to feed our friend, the good wolf. The first step is courage, overcoming the fear that leads to hatred. As I (BA) walked in the footsteps of Nelson Mandela on Robbins Island in South Africa, I had the extraordinary privilege of spending time in one-to-one conversation with a tour guide who had been a prison inmate with Nelson Mandela. We talked about fear, hatred, and the cascade of violence. He showed me where Mandela hid pieces of his manuscript, *The Long Walk to Freedom*, prior to being smuggled out to Lusaka, Zambia and then to London for publication. He reminded me of these words by his former cellmate Nelson Mandela: "The brave man is not he who does not feel afraid but he who conquers that fear."

References

Aalerding, Hillie; Femke S. Ten Velden; Gerben A. van Kleef; Karsten K. W. De Dreu. 2018. "Parochial Cooperation in Nested Intergroup Dilemmas Is Reduced When It Harms Out-Groups." *Journal of Personality and Social Psychology* 114:909–923.

Abrams, Lindsay. 2015. "Big Oil's Decades of Deception: Report Reveals That Exxon's Known the Truth About Climate Science Since 1981." *Salon*, July 8, http://www.salon.com/2015/07/08/big_oils_decades_of_deception_report_reveals_that_exxons_known_the_truth_about_climate_science_since_1981/

Acharya, Avidit; Matthew Blackwell; Maya Sen. 2018. *Deep Roots: How Slavery Still Shapes Southern Politics*. Princeton: Princeton University Press.

Agamben, Giorgio. 2004. *State of Exception*. Translated by Kevin Attell. Chicago: University of Chicago Press.

Agyekumwaa, Akua. 2016. *Hurt People Hurt People: Breaking the Vicious Cycle of Abuse*. CreateSpace Independent Publishing Platform.

Ahmed, Nafeez. 2019. "How US Climate Deniers Are Working with Far-Right Racists to Hijack Brexit for Big Oil." *Le Monde Diplomatique*, June, https://mondediplo.com/outsidein/brexit-climate-deniers

Allport, Gordon. 1954. *The Nature of Prejudice*. Cambridge, MA: Addison-Wesley.

Altemeyer, Bob. 2010. "Highly Dominating, Highly Authoritarian Personalities." *Journal of Social Psychology* 144:421–448.

Alvarez, Alex, and Ronet Bachman. 2017. *Violence: The Enduring Problem*. 3rd edn. Sage.

Ames, Daniel, and Susan T. Fiske. 2015. "Perceived Intent Motivates People to Magnify Observed Harms." *Proceedings of the National Academy of Sciences* 112:3599–3605.

Amnesty International. 2011. *Deadly Delivery: The Maternal Health Care Crisis in the USA: One-Year Update*. New York, NY: Amnesty International Publications, https://cdn2.sph.harvard.edu/wp-content/uploads/sites/32/2017/06/deadlydelivery oneyear.pdf

Amrith, Sunil. 2018. *Unruly Waters: How Rains, Rivers, Coasts, and Seas Have Shaped Asian History*. New York: Basic Books.

Andersen, Kurt. 2017. "How America Lost Its Mind." *Atlantic*, Sept., https://ww w.theatlantic.com/magazine/archive/2017/09/how-america-lost-its-mind/534231/ ?utm_source=fbb

Anderson (Frye), Barbara. 1995. "Diversity in the Family Forum." In *Make Us One*, Delbert Baker, ed. Boise, ID: Pacific Press Publishing Association. Pp. 139–158.

Anderson, Barbara, and Lisa Roberts. 2019. *The Maternal Health Crisis in America: Nursing Implications for Advocacy and Practice*. New York: Springer Publishing Co.

Anderson, E. N. 2010. *The Pursuit of Ecotopia*. Santa Barbara, CA: ABC-Clio.

———. 2011. "Drawing from Traditional and 'Indigenous' Socioecological Theories." In *Environmental Anthropology Today*, Helen Kopnina and Eleanor Shoreman-Ouimet, eds. London: Routledge. Pp. 56–74.

———. 2014. *Everyone Eats*. 2nd edn. New York: New York University Press.

———. 2019. *The East Asian World-System: Climate Change and Dynastic Cycles*. Springer Publishing Co.

Anderson, E. N., and Barbara A. Anderson. 2013. *Warning Signs of Genocide: An Anthropological Perspective*. Lanham, Maryland: Lexington Books.

———. 2017. *Halting Genocide in America: An Anthropological Perspective*. Chesterfield, MO: Mira Publishing.

Anderson, Kjell. 2015. "Colonialism and Cold Genocide: The Case of West Papua." *Genocide Studies and Prevention* 9:9–25.

Anderton, Charles, and Jurgen Brauer. 2019. "The Onset, Spread, and Prevention of Mass Atrocities: Perspectives from Formal Network Models." *Journal of Genocide Research* 21:481–503.

Applebaum, Anne. 2017. *Red Famine: Stalin's War on Ukraine*. New York: Penguin/ Random House.

Arendt, Hannah. 1963. *Eichmann in Jerusalem: A Report on the Banality of Evil*. New York: Viking.

Aristotle. 1953. *The Ethics of Aristotle*. Translated by J. A. K. Thomson. New York: Penguin.

Atran, Scott. 2010. *Talking to the Enemy: Faith, Brotherhood, and the (Un)Making of Terrorists*. New York: HarperCollins.

———. 2015. "Response to a Request for Recommendations to the UN Security Council Committee on Counter Terrorism." *Journal of Political Risk* 3:12, file:///C: /Users/owner/Downloads/Atran%20on%20what%20to%20do.html

Auzanneau, Mattheiu. 2018. *Oil, Power, and War: A Dark History*. Translated by John F. Reynolds. Corvallis, OR and White River Junction, VT: Post Carbon Institute and Chelsea Green Publishing.

Azarian, Bobby. 2019. "A Complete Psychological Analysis of Trump's Support." *Psychology Today*.

Bandura, Albert. 1982. "Self-Efficacy Mechanism in Human Agency." *American Psychologist* 37:122–147.

———. 1986. *Social Foundations of Thought and Action: A Social Cognitive Theory*. Englewood Cliffs, NJ: Prentice-Hall.

———. 2016. *Moral Disengagement: How People Do Harm and Live with Themselves*. New York: Worth Publishers, MacMillan Learning.

Barkun, Michael. 2013. *A Culture of Conspiracy: Apocalyptic Visions in Contemporary America*. 2nd edn. Berkeley: University of California Press.

Baron-Cohen, Simon. 2011. *Zero Degrees of Empathy: A New Theory of Human Cruelty*. London: Allen Lane. In US As: *The Science of Evil: On Empathy and the Origins of Cruelty*. New York: Basic Books.

Bartlett, Steven James. 2005. *The Pathology of Man: A Study of Human Evil*. Springfield, IL: Charles C. Thomas.

Baskin-Sommers, Arielle; Allison M. Stuppy-Sullivan; Joshua W. Buckholz. 2016. "Psychopathic Individuals Exhibit but Do Not Avoid Regret During Counterfactual Decision-Making." *Proceedings of the National Academy of Sciences* 113:14438–14443.

Batson, Daniel. 2011. *Altruism in Humans*. Oxford: Oxford University Press.

Bauer, Michal; Jana Cahliková; Julie Chytilová; Tomáš Želinsky. 2018. "Social Contagion of Ethnic Hostility." *Proceedings of the National Academy of Sciences* 115:4881–4886.

Baumeister, Roy. 1997. *Evil: Inside Human Violence and Cruelty*. San Francisco: W. H. Freeman.

Baumeister, Roy F.; Laura Smart; Joseph M. Boden. 1996. "Relation of Threatened Egotism to Violence and Aggression: The Dark Side of High Self-Esteem." *Psychological Review* 103:5–33.

Beals, Alan R., and Bernard J. Siegel. 1966. *Divisiveness and Social Conflict: An Anthropological Approach*. Stanford: Stanford University Press.

Beauchamp, Zack. 2018. "Study: 24 Million Americans Think Like the Alt-Right." *Vox*, August 10, https://www.vox.com/2018/8/10/17670992/study-white-amer icans-alt-right-racism-white-nationalists

Beck, Aaron. 1999. *Prisoners of Hate: The Cognitive Basis of Anger, Hostility, and Violence*. New York: HarperCollins.

Beckford, George L. 1972. *Persistent Poverty: Underdevelopment in Plantation Economies of the Third World*. New York: Oxford University Press.

Bélanger, Jocelyn J.; Julie Caouette; Keren Sharvit; Michelle Dugas. 2014. "The Psychology of Martyrdom: Making the Ultimate Sacrifice in the Name of a Cause." *Journal of Personality and Social Psychology* 107:494–515.

Besteman, Catherine. 2019. "Militarized Global Apartheid." *Current Anthropology* 60: Supplement 19:S26–S38.

Bilewicz, Michal. 2020. "Obedient Authoritarians or Lay Darwinists?" In *Confronting Humanity at Its Worst: Social Psychological Perspective on Genocide*, Leonard S. Newman, ed. Oxford and New York: Oxford University Press. Pp. 29–61.

Biran, Michal. 2005. *The Empire of the Qara Khitai in Eurasian History: Between China and the Islamic World*. Cambridge: Cambridge University Press.

Blum, Ben. 2018. "The Lifespan of a Lie." *Medium*, June 7, https://medium.com/s/ trustissues/the-lifespan-of-a-lie-d869212b1f62

Boehm, Christopher. 1999. *Hierarchy in the Forest*. Cambridge, MA: Harvard University Press.

Bourdieu, P. 1991. *The Political Ontology of Martin Heidegger.* Translated by Peter Collier. Stanford: Stanford University Press.

Bowles, Samuel. 2006. "Group Competition, Reproductive Leveling, and the Evolution of Human Altruism." *Science* 314:1569–1572.

———. 2008. "Conflict: Altruism's Midwife." *Nature* 456:326–327.

———. 2009. "Did Warfare Among Ancestral Hunter-Gatherers Affect the Evolution of Human Social Behaviors?" *Science* 324:1293–1298.

Bowles, Samuel, and Herbert Gintis. 2011. *A Cooperative Species: Human Reciprocity and Its Evolution.* Princeton: Princeton University Press.

Boyer, Pascal. 2018. *Minds Make Societies: How Cognitions Explains the World Humans Create.* New Haven: Yale University Press.

Brandt, Richard B. 1979. *A Theory of the Good and the Right.* New York: Oxford University Press.

———. 1992. *Morality, Utilitarianism, and Rights.* Cambridge: Cambridge University Press.

———. 1996. *Facts, Values, and Morality.* Cambridge: Cambridge University Press.

Brown, Dee. 1971. *Bury My Heart at Wounded Knee: An Indian History of the American West.* New York: Holt, Rinehart and Winston.

Browning, Christopher R. 2018. "The Suffocation of Democracy." *New York Review of Books,* October 25, https://mail.google.com/mail/u/0/#inbox/FMfcgxvzKtW gjBJltLPfDjrHQfZMrwQc

Byler, Darren. 2018. "China's Government Has Ordered a Million Citizens to Occupy Uighur Homes. Here's What They Think They Are Doing." *Chinafile,* October 24, http://www.chinafile.com/reporting-opinion/postcard/million-citizens-occupy -uighur-homes-xinjiang?fbclid=IwAR0oiTYptmpsLovi8SMaCMM8DJzLPwDcg ktHRqzbWjPCMCo2c5_8J8JcHmA

Cahill, Tom. 2017. "Here's How Much Exxon Paid Republicans Who Urged Trump to Ditch Climate Deal." *Resistance Report,* June 1, http://resistancereport.com/po litics/exxon-paid-republicans-paris/

Cai, Weiyi; Troy Griggs; Jason Gao; Juliette Love; Joe Ward. 2019. "White Extremist Ideology Drives Many Deadly Shootings." *New York Times,* August 4, https:// www.nytimes.com/interactive/2019/08/04/us/white-extremist-active-shooter.html ?action=clickandmodule=Top%20Storiesandpgtype=Homepage

Cameron, Catherine M.; Paul Kelton; Alan C. Swedlund (eds.). 2015. *Beyond Germs: Native Depopulation in North America.* Tucson: University of Arizona Press.

Cameron, Hazel. 2018. "State-Organized Starvation: A Weapon of Extreme Mass Violence in Matabeleland South, 1984." *Genocide Studies International* 12:26–47.

Caprara, Gian V. 2002. Review of *Prisoners of Hate* by Aaron Beck. *Contemporary Psychology/APA Review of Books* 47:180–184.

Case, Anne, and Angus Deaton. 2015. "Rising Morbidity and Mortality in Midlife Among White Non-Hispanic Americans in the 21st Century." *Proceedings of the National Academy of Sciences* 112:15078–15083.

———. 2020. *Deaths of Despair and the Future of Capitalism.* Princeton: Princeton University Press.

Castano, Emanuele. 2012. "Antisocial Behavior in Individuals and Groups." In *The Oxford Handbook of Personality and Social Psychology*, Kay Deaux and Mark Snyder, eds. New York: Oxford University Press. Pp. 419–445.

Cattaneo, Lauren Bennett, and Aliya R. Chapman. 2010. "The Process of Empowerment: A Model for Use in Research and Practice." *American Psychologist* 65:646–659.

Checks and Balances Project. 2017. "Koch Brothers' Growing Control Extends to 18 Departments." *Checks and Balances Project, Investigative Watchdog Project*, July 5, https://checksandbalancesproject.org/koch-strength-increases/?fbclid=IwAR2uSWFvZBcjU39XLs_6jOx-qjPx6bwNYICdcKeVvYSD9UDSGopwrNjKHIs

Chenoweth, Erica, and Maria Stephan. 2012. *Why Civil Resistance Works*. New York: Columbia University Press.

Cheung, Maria; Torsten Trey; David Matas; Richard An. 2018. "Cold Genocide: Falun Gong in China." *Genocide Studies and Prevention* 12:38–62.

Choi, Donghyun Danny; Mathias Portner; Nicolas Sambanis. 2019. "Parochialism, Social Norms, and Discrimination Against Immigrants." *Proceedings of the National Academy of Sciences* 116:16274–16279.

Choi, Jung-Kyoo, and Samuel Bowles. 2007. "The Coevolution of Parochial Altruism and War." *Science* 318:636–640.

Christian, David. 2004. *Maps of Time: An Introduction to Big History*. Berkeley: University of California Press. New Preface, 2011.

Chuang, Frank; Ed Manley; Arthur Petersen. 2020. "The Role of Worldviews in the Governance of Sustainable Mobility." *Proceedings of the National Academy of Sciences* 117:4034–4042.

Clutton-Brock, Tim. 2016. *Mammal Societies*. New York: Wiley Blackwell.

Coady, David; Ian Parry; Louis Sears; Baoping Shang. 2017. "How Large Are Global Fossil Fuel Subsidies?" *World Development* 91:11–27.

Collier, Paul, and Nicholas Sambanis. 2005. *Understanding Civil War: Evidence and Analysis*. 2 vol. Washington, DC: World Bank.

Columbia University Irving Medical Center. 2019. "Bone, Not Adrenaline, Drives Fight or Flight Response." *PhysOrg*, Sept. 12, https://phys.org/news/2019-09-bone-adrenaline-flight-response.html?fbclid=IwAR3qy7fUDW6Ubi-XLka6NCwRNh-biyODrF9nVO0pxbTg_emiE1pGKl8T8LE

Copeland, William; Dieter Wolke; Suzet Tanya Lereya; Lilly Shanahan; Carol Worthman; E. Jane Costello. 2014. "Childhood Bullying Involvement Predicts Low-Grade Systemic Inflammation into Adulthood." *Proceedings of the National Academy of Sciences* 111:7570–7575.

Council on Foreign Relations. 2019. *Modern Slavery: Its Root Causes and the Human Toll* [Online presentation]. Posted by *Council on Foreign Relations*, October 17, https://www.cfr.org/interactives/modern-slavery/?utm_medium=social_ownedand utm_source=fbandutm_campaign=modern-slaveryandutm_content=101719andfbclid=IwAR3liNVOwm3K647DO5FxwsGHdtEd7k-u0Xv3fBKl1CVg_2N6I8N79UGCRP4#!/section1/item-1

Curry, Oliver Scott; Daniel Austin Mullins; Harvey Whitehouse. 2019. "Is It Good to Cooperate? Testing the Theory of Morality-As-Cooperation in 60 Societies." *Current Anthropology* 60:47–69.

Dadds, Mark R., and Lucy A. Tully. 2019. "What Is It to Discipline a Child: What Should It Be? A Reanalysis of Time-Out from the Perspective of Child Mental Health, Attachment, and Trauma." *American Psychologist* 74:794–808.

De Becker, Gavin. 1997. *The Gift of Fear*. New York: Random House.

De Dreu, Karsten K. W.; Jŏrg Gross; Zsomber Méder; Michael Giffin; Eliska Prochazkova; Jonathan Krikeb; Simon Columbus. 2016. "In-Group Defense, Out-Group Aggression, and Coordination Failures in Intergroup Conflict." *Proceedings of the American Academy of Sciences* 113:10524–10529.

de Waal, Frans. 1996. *Good Natured: The Origins of Right and Wrong in Humans and Other Animals*. Cambridge, MA: Harvard University Press.

Denworth, Lydia. 2017. "I Feel Your Pain." *Scientific American*, December, 58–63.

Dikötter, Frank. 2019. *How to Be a Dictator: The Cult of Personality in the Twentieth Century*. London: Bloomsbury.

Ding, Yu, and Krishna Savani. 2020. "From Variability to Vulnerability: People Exposed to Greater Variability Judge Wrongdoers More Harshly." *Journal of Personality and Social Psychology* 188:1101–1117.

Duckitt, John. 1994. *The Social Psychology of Prejudice*. New York: Praeger.

———. 2001. "A Dual-Process Cognitive-Motivational Theory of Ideology and Prejudice." In *Advances in Experimental Social Psychology*. Academic Press. Pp. 41–113.

Dulin, John. 2017. "Transvaluing ISIS in Orthodox Christian-Majority Ethiopia: On the Inhibition of Group Violence." *Current Anthropology* 58:785–804.

Dunbar, Robin. 2010. *How Many Friends Does One Person Need? Dunbar's Number and Other Evolutionary Quirks*. Cambridge, MA: Harvard University Press.

Durkheim, Emile. 1995 [1912]. *The Elementary Forms of Religious Life*. Translated by Karen E. Fields. New York: Free Press.

Edelman, Marian Wright. 1994. *The Measure of Our Success*. Boston: Beacon Press.

Eisinger, Jesse. 2017. *The Chickenshit Club: Why the Justice Department Fails to Prosecute Executives*. New York: Simon and Schuster.

Ellis, Albert. 1962. *Reason and Emotion in Psychotherapy*. New York: Citadel.

Ellsmoor, James. 2019. "U.S. Spend Ten Times More on Fossil Fuel Subsidies than on Education." *Forbes*, June 15, https://www.forbes.com/sites/jamesellsmoor/20 19/06/15/united-states-spend-ten-times-more-on-fossil-fuel-subsidies-than-educat ion/?fbclid=IwAR1D1nxoOs1mczovgR6Xm7cWHh0aoUcM7COcc4yuAo1rAn SRKP8maHloMEA#2283014c4473

Falk, Dean, and Charles Hildebolt. 2017. "Annual War Deaths in Small-Scale Versus State Societies Scale with Population Size Rather Than Violence." *Current Anthropology* 58:805–813.

Fattal, Alexander L. 2019. "Target Intimacy: Notes on the Convergence of the Militarization and Marketization of Love in Colombia." *Current Anthropology* 60: Supplement 19:S49–S61.

Fein, Helen. 2007. *Human Rights and Wrongs: Slavery, Terror, Genocide.* London: Paradigm.

Feinberg, Matthew; Elisabeth Wehling; Joanne M. Chung; Laura R. Saslow; Ingrid Melvaer Paulin. 2020. "Measuring Moral Politics: How Strict and Nurturant Family Values Explain Individual Differences in Conservatism, Liberalism, and the Political Middle." *Journal of Personality and Social Psychology* 118:777–804.

Festinger, Leon; Henry W. Riecken; Stanley Schachter. 1956. *When Prophecy Fails.* New York: Harper and Row.

Fields, R. Douglas. 2019. "The Roots of Human Aggression." *Scientific American,* May, 64–71.

Fiske, Alan Page, and Tage Shakti Rai. 2014. *Virtuous Violence: Hurting and Killing to Create, Sustain, End, and Honor Social Relationships.* Cambridge: Cambridge University Press.

Fletcher, Joseph. 1980. "Turko-Mongolian Monarchic Tradition in the Ottoman Empire." *Harvard Ukrainian Studies* 3–4(1979–1980):1:236–251.

Folley, Aris. 2019. "Top Oil Firms Have Spent $1B on Branding, Lobbying Since Paris Agreement: Study." *The Hill,* March 27, https://thehill.com/policy/energy -environment/436117-top-oil-firms-spend-millions-on-lobbying-to-block-climate -change?fbclid=IwAR1wwz9Hux7nKsxU32BWkcX22aV0X6J_eKfIhorwO2z xk87ucFhUOI1Hf4Y

Forscher, Patrick S., and Nour S. Kteily. 2020. "A Psychological Profile of the Alt-Right." *Perspectives on Psychological Science* 15:90–116.

Frankl, Viktor. 1959. *Man's Search for Meaning: An Introduction to Logotherapy.* Boston: Beacon.

———. 1978. *The Unheard Cry for Meaning: Psychotherapy and Humanism.* New York: Simon and Schuster.

———. 2019. *Yes to Life: In Spite of Everything.* Boston, MA: Beacon Press.

Friedman, Ann. 2017. "Embrace the Sweet Bliss of Ignorance." *Los Angeles Times,* Deccember 20, A13.

Friedman, Lisa, and Claire O'Neill. 2020. "Who Controls Trump's Environmental Policy?" *New York Times,* January 14, https://www.nytimes.com/interactive/2020 /01/14/climate/fossil-fuel-industry-environmental-policy.html?fbclid=IwAR1K ttMDeGql15KIlSZth-w_QgpHR_Wx86hJEcpd_yM-x1AYWdH8jYW3jBU

Fromm, Erich. 1941. *Escape from Freedom.* New York: Farrar and Rinehart.

Fry, Douglas P. (ed.). 2013. *War, Peace, and Human Nature: The Convergence of Evolutionary and Cultural Views.* New York: Oxford University Press.

Fukuyama, Francis. 2016. "America: The Failed State." *Prospect Magazine,* December 13, http://www.prospectmagazine.co.uk/magazine/america-the-failed -state-donald-trump

Gabbert, Wolfgang. 2019. *Violence and the Caste War of Yucatán.* Cambridge: Cambridge University Press.

Galtung, Johan. 1969. Violence, Peace, and Peace Research. *Journal of Peace Research* 6:3:167–191.

Gertz, Matt. 2017. "Breitbart Is Not Independent, It's the Communications Arm of the Mercers' Empire." *MediaMatters,* April 21, https://mediamatters.org/research

/2017/04/21/breitbart-not-independent-its-communications-arm-mercers-empire/2
16128

Gibbon, Edward. 1995 [1776–1788]. *The Decline and the Fall of the Roman Empire.*
New York: Penguin.

Giddens, Anthony. 1984. *The Constitution of Society.* Berkeley, CA: University of
California Press.

Gigerenzer, Gerd. 2007. *Gut Feelings: The Intelligence of the Unconscious.* New
York: Viking.

Gigerenzer, Gerd; Peter M. Todd; The ABC [Adaptive Behavior and Cognition]
Research Group. 1999. *Simple Heuristics That Make Us Smart.* Oxford: Oxford
University Press.

Goffman, Erving. 1963. *Stigma: Notes on the Management of Spoiled Identity.*
Englewood Cliffs, NJ: Prentice-Hall.

Goitein, Elizabeth. 2019. "What the President Could Do If He Declares a State of
Emergency." *The Atlantic*, January–February, https://www.theatlantic.com/ma
gazine/archive/2019/01/presidential-emergency-powers/576418/?fbclid=IwAR0r9
sHrMY3rflhWKSrb9-1gSSGUq-kj6vl7QZS3pEbUvxhIcV8QVoC18Zg.

Goldhagen, Daniel. 1996. *Hitler's Willing Executioners: Ordinary Germans and the
Holocaust.* New York: Random House.

González-Forero, Mauricio, and Andy Gardner. 2018. "Inference of Ecological and
Social Drivers of Human Brain-Size Evolution." *Nature* 557:554–557.

Graeber, David. 2014. *Debt—Updated and Expanded: The First 5,000 Years.* New
York: Melville House.

Graeber, David, and David Wengrow. 2018. "How to Change the Course of History
(At Least, the Part That's Already Happened)." *Eurozine*, March 2, file:///C:/User
s/user/Downloads/Graeber%20and%20Wengrow%20on%20society.html

Grandia, Liza. 2012. *Enclosed: Conservation, Cattle, and Commerce Among the
Q'eqchi' Maya Lowlanders.* Seattle: University of Washington Press.

Green, Joshua. 2017. *Devil's Bargain: Steve Bannon, Donald Trump, and the
Storming of the Presidency.* New York: Penguin.

Greenaway, Katharine H., and Tegan Cruwys. 2019. "The Source Model of Group
Threat: Responding to Internal and External Threats." *American Psychologist*
74:218–231.

Griscom, Bronson; Justin Adams; Peter Ellis; Richard Houghton; Guy Lomax;
Daniela A. Miteva; William H. Schlesinger; D. Shoch; J. V. Siikamäki; P. Smith;
P. Woodbury. 2017. "Natural Climate Solutions." *Proceedings of the National
Academy of Sciences* 114:11645–11650.

Guichaoua, André. 2020. "Counting the Rwandan Victims of War and Genocide:
Concluding Remarks." *Journal of Genocide Research* 22:125–141.

Guimond, Serge; Richard J. Crisp; Pierre De Oliveira; Rodolphe Kamiejski; Nour
Kteily; Beate Kuepper; Richard N. Lalonde; S. Levin; F. Pratto; F. Tougas; J.
Sidanius. 2013. "Diversity Policy, Social Dominance, and Intergroup Relations:
Predicting Prejudice in Changing Social and Political Contexts." *Journal of
Personality and Social Psychology* 104:941–958.

Gusterson, Hugh. 2019. "Drone Warfare in Waziristan and the New Military Humanism." *Current Anthropology* 60: Supplement 19:S77–S86.

Gusterson, Hugh, and Catherine Besteman. 2019. "Cultures of Militarism: An Introduction to Supplement 19." *Current Anthropology* 60: Supplement 19:S3–S14.

Habermas, Jürgen. 1987. *The Theory of Communicative Action.* 2 vol. Translated by Thomas McCarthy. German Original 1981. Boston: Beacon.

Hahl, Oliver; Minjae Kim; Ezra W. Zuckerman Sivan. 2018. "The Authentic Appeal of the Lying Demagogue: Proclaiming the Deeper Truth About Political Illegitimacy." *American Sociological Review* 83:1–33.

Haidt, Jonathan. 2012. *The Righteous Mind: Why Good People Are Divided by Politics and Religion.* New York: Pantheon.

Hämäläinen, Pekka. 2008. *The Comanche Empire.* New Haven: Yale University Press.

Hammami, Rema. 2019. "Destabilizing Mastery and the Machine: Palestinian Agency and Gendered Embodiment at Israeli Military Checkpoints." *Current Anthropology* 60: Supplement 19:S87–S97.

Harff, Barbara. 2012. "Assessing Risks of Genocide and Politicide: A Global Watch List for 2012." In *Peace and Conflict 2012*, J. Joseph Hewitt, Jonathan Wilkenfeld, and Ted Robert Gurr, eds. Boulder, CO: Paradigm Press. Pp. 53–56.

Harris, Judith Rich. 1998. *The Nurture Assumption: Why Children Turn Out the Way They Do.* New York: Free Press.

Harvey, Fiona; Damian Carrington; Jonathan Watts; Patrick Greenfield. 2019. "How Do We Rein in the Fossil Fuel Industry? Here Are Eight Ideas." *The Guardian*, October. 14, https://www.theguardian.com/environment/2019/oct/14/how-rein-in-f ossil-fuel-industry-eight-ideas?fbclid=IwAR007mkRyZU9Gtg60sXH6dj1WlMs0 c4ZVg8BIimJWTf7RROjbCcXa56mAMQ

Haslam, Nick. 2006. "Dehumanization: An Integrative Review. *Personality and Social Psychology Review* 10:252–264.

———. 2020. "The Many Roles of Dehumanization in Genocide." In *Confronting Humanity at Its Worst: Social Psychological Perspective on Genocide*, Leonard S. Newman, ed. Oxford and New York: Oxford University Press. Pp. 119–138.

Haslam, S. Alexander; Stephen D. Reicher; Jay J. Van Bavel. 2019. "Rethinking the Nature of Cruelty: The Role of Identity Leadership in the Stanford Prison Experiment." *American Psychologist* 74:809–822.

Hawken, Paul (ed.). 2017. *Drawdown: The Most Comprehensive Plan Ever Proposed to Reverse Global Warming.* New York: Penguin.

Hawley, Emily. 2018. "ISIS Crimes Against the Shia: The Islamic State's Genocide Against Shia Muslims." *Genocide Studies International* 11:160–181.

Hayes, Susan L.; David C. Radley; Douglas McCarthy. 2018. "States of Despair: A Closer Look at Rising State Death Rates from Drugs, Alcohol, and Suicide." *Commonwealth Fund, To the Point Blog*, August 9, https://www.commonwealthf und.org/blog/2018/states-despair-closer-look-rising-state-death-rates-drugs-alco hol-and-suicide?utm_source=states-despair-closer-look-rising-state-death-rates-d rugs-alcohol-and-suicideandutm_medium=Facebookandutm_campaign=Health+C overage

Healy, Melissa. 2018. "No Lie: Voters Tolerate Politicians' Fibs." *Los Angeles Times*, December 24, A5.

Heid, Markham. 2019. "The Roots of Good and Evil." In *The Roots of Good and Evil, Special TIME Edition*. Pp. 16–23.

Heinberg, Richard. 2017. "Energy and Authoritarianism." http://energyskeptic.com/2018/richard-heinberg-energy-and-authoritarianism/

Hemming, John. 1978. *Red Gold: The Conquest of the Brazilian Indians*. London: MacMillan.

Henrich, Joseph. 2016. *The Secret of Our Success: How Culture Is Driving Human Evolution, Domesticating Our Species, and Making Us Smarter*. Princeton: Princeton University Press.

Henry, P. J. 2009. "Low-Status Compensation: A Theory for Understanding the Role of Status in Cultures of Honor." *Journal of Personality and Social Psychology* 97:451–466.

Hesse, Hermann. 2002. *Steppenwolf*. Translated by Basil Creighton. German Original 1927. London: Picador.

Hobbes, Michael. 2020. "The Golden Age of White Collar Crime." *Huffpost*, February 10, https://www.huffpost.com/highline/article/white-collar-crime/?utm_campaign=hp_fb_pagesandutm_medium=facebookandutm_source=politics_fbandsection=politicsandncid=fcbklnkushpmg00000013andfbclid=IwAR3QLaQmG6xlYL9WrDPYSUpjWQ0lvdHHF58x-9AVgkKCb9KykL6FniIiUds

Hobbes, Thomas. 1950 [1651]. *Leviathan*. New York: Dutton.

Hope, Mat. 2019. "Revealed: How the Tobacco and Fossil Fuel Companies Fund Disinformation Campaigns Throughout the World." *Desmogblog*, February 19, https://www.desmogblog.com/2019/02/19/how-tobacco-and-fossil-fuel-companies-fund-disinformation-campaigns-around-world?fbclid=IwAR0oI640hIv9HYUrCf0AUCJKIgrqPaWfH5JHp5H5tfSGNEPyybEkAlrH71o

Hostinar, Camelia E., and Gregory E. Miller. 2019. "Protective Factors for Youth Confronting Economic Hardship: Current Challenges and Future Avenues in Resilience Research." *American Psychologist* 74:641–652.

Howard-Hassman, Rhoda E. 2016. *State Food Crimes*. Cambridge: Cambridge University Press.

Hume, David. 1969 [1739–1740]. *A Treatise of Human Nature*. New York: Penguin.

Huxley, Aldous. 1932. B*rave New World*. New York: Harper Brothers.

Joeden-Forgey, Elisa von, and Thomas McGee. 2019. "Editors' Introduction: Palimpsestic Genocide in Kurdistan." *Genocide Studies International* 13:1–9.

Johnston, David Cay. 2007. *Free Lunch: How the Richest Americans Enrich Themselves at Government Expense (and Stick You with the Bill)*. New York: Penguin.

Kachanoff, Frank J.; Donald M. Taylor; Thomas H. Khullar; Julie Caouette; Michael J. A. Wohl. 2019. "The Chains on All My People Are the Chains on Me: Restrictions to Collective Autonomy Undermine the Personal Autonomy and Psychological Well-Being of Group Members." *Journal of Personality and Social Psychology* 116:141–165.

Kahneman, Daniel. 2011. *Thinking, Fast and Slow*. New York: Farrar, Straus and Giroux.

Kant, Immanuel. 2002. *Groundwork for the Metaphysics of Morals*. Edited and Translated by Allen W. Wood. German Original 1785. New Haven: Yale University Press.

Kaufman, Scott Barry. 2018. "The One Personality Trait That Is Ripping America (and the World) Apart." *Scientific American*, October 26, https://blogs.scient ificamerican.com/beautiful-minds/the-one-personality-trait-that-is-ripping-america -and-the-world-apart/?fbclid=IwAR0kZdrrSVC3UCRamGkHdVFDAKLG2Hm0 0PDCcHS8OGdvbYHl5ZYC_8kpW7Q

Keeley, Lawrence. 1996. *War Before Civilization*. New York: Oxford University Press.

Keneally, Thomas. 1982. *Schindler's List*. New York: Simon and Schuster, Inc.

Khaldun, Ibn. 1958. *The Muqaddimah*. Translated by Franz Rosenthal. New York: Pantheon.

Kiernan, Ben. 2007. *Blood and Soil: A World History of Genocide and Extermination from Sparta to Darfur*. New Haven: Yale University Press.

Kidder, John Tracey. 2009. *Strength in What Remains*. New York: Random House.

Kincaid, John D. 2016. "The Rational Basis of Irrational Politics: Examining the Great Texas Political Shift to the Right." *Politics and Society* 44:525–550.

Kirby, Alex. 2017. "Taxpayers Give Billions in Fossil Fuel Subsidies, Lose Trillions to Related Health Costs." *EcoWatch*, July 25, https://www.ecowatch.com/fossil -fuel-subsidies-2467529956.html

Kissel, Marc, and Nam Kim. 2018. "The Emergence of Human Warfare: Current Perspectives." *American Journal of Physical Anthropology* 168:doi.org/10.1002/ ajpa.23751.

Klaas, Brian. 2017. *The Despot's Apprentice: Donald Trump's Attack on Democracy*. New York: Hot Books.

Klein, Naomi. 2007. *The Shock Doctrine*. New York: Metropolitan Books (Henry Holt).

———. 2014. *This Changes Everything: Capitalism vs. the Climate*. New York: Simon and Schuster.

Kliff, Sarah. 2018. "American Kids 70% More Likely to Die Before Adulthood than Kids in Other Rich Countries." *Vox*, Jan. 8, https://www.vox.com/health-care/201 8/1/8/16863656/childhood-mortality-united-states?fbclid=IwAR2M3kEcEBusv _0Y3Pgxoz4MiuoaoWAe0kV7UdUcP2lW1fqsaPMc0XOvIfo

Kluger, Jeffrey; Tiffany Sharples; Alexandra Silver. 2019. "What Makes Us Moral." In *The Science of Good and Evil: Special TIME Edition*. Pp. 6–15.

Kofta, Mirosław; Wiktor Soral; Michał Bilewicz. 2020. "What Breeds Conspiracy Antisemitism? The Role of Political Uncontrollability and Uncertainty in the Belief in Jewish Conspiracy." *Journal of Personality and Social Psychology* 118:900–918.

Kohrman, Matthew; Gan Quan; Liu Wennan; Robert N. Proctor (eds.). 2018. *Poisonous Pandas: Chinese Cigarette Manufacturing in Critical Historical Perspectives*. Stanford: Stanford University Press.

Kopnina, Helen, and Eleanor Shoreman-Ouimet (eds.). 2011. *Environmental Anthropology Today*. London: Routledge.

Korsgaard, Christine M. 1996. *Creating the Kingdom of Ends*. Cambridge: Cambridge University Press.

Kroodsma, David A.; Juan Mayorga; Timothy Hochberg; Nathan A. Miller; Kristina Boerder; Francesco Ferretti; Alex Wilson; Bjorn Bergman; Timothy D. White; Barbara A. Block; Paul Woods; Brian Sullivan; Christopher Costello; Boris Worm. 2018. "Tracking the Global Footprint of Fisheries." *Science* 359:904–908.

Kteily, Nour; Emile Bruneau; Adam Waytz; Sarah Cotterill. 2015. "The Ascent of Man; Theoretical and Empirical Evidence for Blatant Dehumanization." *Journal of Personality and Social Psychology* 109:901–931.

Kteily, Nour; Gordon Hodson; Emile Bruneau. 2016. "They See Us As Less Than Human: Metadehumanization Predicts Intergroup Conflict via Reciprocal Dehumanization." *Journal of Personality and Social Psychology* 110:343–370.

Kubler-Ross, Elizabeth. 2014. *On Death and Dying: What the Dying Have to Teach Doctors, Nurses, Clergy and Their Own Families*. 50th anniversary ed. New York: Scribner.

Kummer, Frank. 2018. "$2 Billion Spent to Influence Congress on Climate Change, Drexel Study Finds." *Philadelphia Inquirer*, July 25, http://www.philly.com/phi lly/health/2-billion-spent-to-influence-congress-on-climate-change-drexel-study-finds-20180725.html

Kyle, Sarah R. 2017. *Medicine and Humanism in Late Medieval Italy: The Carrara Herbal in Padua*. London: Routledge Taylor and Francis.

Lachmann, Richard. 2020. *First Class Passengers on a Sinking Ship: Elite Politics and the Decline of Great Powers*. London: Verso.

Lang, Samantha F., and Blaine J. Fowers. 2019. "An Expanded Theory of Alzheimer's Caregiving." *American Psychologist* 74:194–206.

Langer, Ellen. 1983. *The Psychology of Control*. Beverly Hills: Sage.

Lauter, David. 2019. "Trump Has Remade GOP, but Poll Finds It's at a Price." *Los Angeles Times*, August 22, A2.

Le Texier, Thibault. 2019. "Debunking the Stanford Prison Experiment." *American Psychologist* 74:823–839.

LeDoux, Joseph. 2015. *Anxious: Using the Brain to Understand and Trust Fear and Anxiety*. New York: Viking.

Lefebvre, Henri. 1992. *The Production of Space*. French Original 1986. New York: Wiley-Blackwell.

Leonard, Christopher. 2019. *Kochland: The Secret Histories of Koch Industries and Corporate Power in America*. New York: Simon and Schuster.

Lerner, Melvin. 1980. *Belief in a Just World: A Fundamental Delusion*. New York: Plenum.

Lerro, Bruce. 2019. *Lucifer's Labyrinth: Individualism, Hyper-Abstract Thinking, and the Process of Becoming Civilized*. N.p.: Author.

Leung, Angela K., and Dov Cohen. 2011. "Within- and Between-Culture Variation: Individual Differences and the Cultural Logics of Honor, Face, and Dignity Cultures." *Journal of Personality and Social Psychology* 100:507–526.

Leyens, J. P.; P. Paladino; R. Rodriguez-Torres; J. Vaes; S. Demoulin; A. Rodriguez-Perez; G. R. Gaunt. 2000. "The Emotional Side of Prejudice: The Attribution of Secondary Emotions to Ingroups and Outgroups." *Personality and Social Psychology Review* 4:186–197.

Li, Lillian. 2007. *Fighting Famine in North China: State, Market, and Environmental Decline, 1690s–1990s*. Stanford, CA: Stanford University Press.

Li, Mengyao, and Bernhard Leidner. 2020. "Understanding Intergroup Violence and Its Aftermath from Perpetrator and Victim Perspectives." In *Confronting Humanity at Its Worst: Social Psychological Perspective on Genocide*, Leonard S. Newman, ed. Oxford and New York: Oxford University Press. Pp. 159–191.

Lombardi, Lisa. 2019. "Where the Demons Play." In *The Science of Good and Evil, Special TIME Edition*. Pp. 24–29.

Lopez, Ian Haney. 2017. *Dog Whistle Politics: How Coded Racial Appeals Have Reinvented Racism and Wrecked the Middle Class*. New York: Oxford University Press.

Louv, Richard. 2019. *Our Wild Calling: How Connecting with Animals Can Transform Our Lives—and Save Theirs*. Algonquin Books.

Luce, Edward. 2017. *The Retreat of Western Liberalism*. New York: Atlantic Monthly Press.

Lutz, Catherine. 2019. "Bureaucratic Weaponry and the Production of Ignorance in Military Operations on Guam." *Current Anthropology* 60: Supplement 19:S108–S121.

Lyubomirsky, Sonja. 2007. *The How of Happiness: A Scientific Approach to Getting the Life You Want*. New York: Penguin Press.

MacDorman, M. and Declercq, E. 2018. "The Failure of the U.S. Maternal Mortality Reporting and its Impact on Women's Lives." *Birth* 45:105–108.

MacIntyre, Alasdair. 1984. *After Virtue: A Study in Moral Theory*. Notre Dame, IN: Notre Dame University Press.

———. 1988. *Whose Justice? Whose Rationality?* Notre Dame, IN: Notre Dame University Press.

MacLean, Nancy. 2017. *Democracy in Chains: The Deep History of the Radical Right's Stealth Plan for America*. New York: Viking.

Madley, Benjamin. 2016. *An American Genocide: The U.S. and the California Indian Catastrophe, 1846–1873*. Danbury, CT: Westchester Publishing Services.

Mandela, Nelson. 1994. *Long Walk to Freedom: The Autobiography of Nelson Mandela*. London: Little, Brown and Company.

Mann, Michael. 2004. *Fascists*. Cambridge: Cambridge University Press.

———. 2005. *The Dark Side of Democracy: Explaining Ethnic Cleansing*. Cambridge: Cambridge University Press.

———. 2018. "Have Wars and Violence Declined?" *Theoretical Sociology* 47:37–60.

Markowitz, David, and Paul Slovic. 2020. "Social, Psychological, and Demographic Characteristics of Dehumanization Toward Immigrants." *Proceedings of the National Academy of Sciences* 117:9260–9269.

Maslow, Abraham. 1970. *Motivation and Personality*. 2nd edn. Harper and Row.

Mason, Lililiana. 2018. *Uncivil Agreement: How Politics Became Our Identity*. Chicago: University of Chicago Press.

Mayer, Jane. 2016. *Dark Money: The Hidden History of the Billionaires Behind the Rise of the Radical Right*. New York: Doubleday.

Mazzucato, Mariana. 2018. *The Value of Everything: Making and Taking in the Global Economy*. New York: Public Affairs.

McLaren, Karla. 2013. *The Art of Empathy: A Complete Guide to Life's Most Neglected Skill*. Louisville, CO: Sounds True Publishing.

McNeill, John Robert, and William H. McNeill. 2003. *The Human Web: A Bird's-Eye View of Human History*. Norton.

McSweeney, Kendra; Erik A. Nielsen; Matthew J. Taylor; David J. Wrathall; Zoe Pearson; Ophelia Wang; Spencer T. Plumb. 2014. "Drug Policy as Conservation Policy: Narco-Deforestation." *Science* 343:498–490.

Meiches, Benjamin. 2019. *The Politics of Annihilation: A Genealogy of Genocide*. Minneapolis: University of Minnesota Press.

Mencius. 1970. *Mencius*. Translated by D. C. Lau. London: Penguin.

Mencken, Henry Louis. 1949. *A Mencken Chrestomathy*. New York: Random House.

Metcalf, Gilbert E. 2020. "What Should Carbon Cost?" *Scientific American*, June, 62–69.

Metzl, Jonathan M. 2019. *Dying of Whiteness: How the Politics of Racial Resentment Is Killing America's Heartland*. New York: Basic Books.

Michaels, David. 2008. *Doubt Is Their Product: How Industry's Assault on Science Threatens Your Health*. New York: Oxford University Press.

———. 2020. *The Triumph of Doubt: Dark Money and the Science of Deception*. New York: Oxford University Press.

Milgram, Stanley. 1974. *Obedience to Authority: An Experimental View*. New York: Harper and Row.

Miller, Alice. 1983. *For Their Own Good: Hidden Cruelty in Childrearing and the Roots of Violence*. New York: Farrar, Strauss and Giroux.

Miller, Virginia P. 1979. *Uknomno'm: The Yuki Indians of Northern California*. Socorro, NM: Ballena Press.

Mintz, Sidney. 1985. *Sweetness and Power: The Place of Sugar in Modern History*. New York: Penguin.

Monbiot, George. 2019. "Demagogues Thrive by Whipping Up Fury. Here's How to Stop Them." *The Guardian*, October 3, https://www.theguardian.com/co mmentisfree/2019/oct/03/demagogues-fury-violence-outrage-discourse?CMP=fb _guandutm_medium=Socialandutm_source=Facebookandfbclid=IwAR0-WHNr -MQk0FG0LYZpq1H53lR7eYbFFicfSfv76Ci3VdKPoBIaqs0lmt0#Echobox=15 70091915

Montague, John. 1998. *The Book of Irish Verse: Irish Poetry form the Sixth Century to the Present*. New York: Bristol Park Books.

Morris, Ian. 2010. *Why the West Rules...For Now*. New York: Farrar, Straus and Giroux.

Mueller, Allison B., and Linda J. Skitka. 2020. "Moral Courage and Moral Disregard: Different Sides of the Same Coin?" In *Confronting Humanity at Its Worst: Social Psychological Perspective on Genocide*, Leonard S. Newman, ed. Oxford and New York: Oxford University Press. Pp. 139–156.

Mutz, Diana C. 2018. "Status Threat, Not Economic Hardship, Explains the 2016 Presidential Vote." *Proceedings of the National Academy of Sciences* 115:E4330–E4339.

National Research Council and the Institute of Medicine. 2013. *U.S. Health in International Perspective: Shorter Lives, Poorer Health*. Washington, DC: The National Academies Press.

Nelson, Diane M. 2019. "Low Intensities." *Current Anthropology* 60: Supplement 19:S122–S133.

Nesbit, Jeff. 2016. *Poison Tea: How Big Oil and Big Tobacco Invented the Tea Party and Captured the GOP*. New York: St. Martin's.

Neuborne, Burt. 2019. *When at Times the Mob is Swayed: A Citizen's Guide to Defending Our Republic*. New York: New Press.

Newman, Leonard S. (ed.). 2020. *Confronting Humanity at Its Worst: Social Psychological Perspectives on Genocide*. Oxford and New York: Oxford University Press.

Newman, Leonard, and Ralph Erber (eds.). 2002. *Understanding Genocide: The Social Psychology of the Holocaust*. Oxford: Oxford University Press.

Nisbett, Richard, and Dov Cohen. 1996. *Culture of Honor: The Psychology of Violence in the South*. Boulder, CO: Westview.

Nova (Magazine). 2017. "Jeanine Pirro, Alex Jones, and Other Conservatives Call for Civil War if Democrats Succeed in Removing Trump." *Nova*, August 5, http://www.nova-magazine.net/jeanine-pirro-alex-jones-james-woods-conservatives-civil-war-democrats-impeachment-trump/

Nyseth Brehm, Hollie. 2017a. "Re-examining Risk Factors of Genocide." *Journal of Genocide Research* 19:61–87.

———. 2017b. "Subnational Determinants of Killing in Rwanda." *Criminology* 55:5–31.

———. 2020. "Moving Beyond the State: An Imperative for Genocide Prediction." *Genocide Studies and Prevention* 13:64–78.

Oil Change International. 2017. "Taxpayers Charged $7 Billion a Year to Subsidize Fossil Fuels on Public Lands." *Ecowatch*, online, May 24, https://www.ecowatch.com/taypayers-subsidize-public-lands-2420255485.html?utm_campaign=RebelMouseandutm_medium=socialandutm_source=facebookandutm_content=EcoWatch

Oreskes, Naomi, and Erik M. Conway. 2010. *Merchants of Doubt: How a Handful of Scientists Obscured the Truth on Issues from Tobacco Smoke to Global Warming*. New York: Bloomsbury.

Orwell, George. 1950. *1984*. New York: Signet Classics.

Osgood, Charles E.; G. Suci; P. Tannenbaum. 1957. *The Measurement of Meaning*. Urbana, IL: University of Illinois Press.

Otto, Ilona; Jonathan F. Donges; Roger Cremades; Avit Bhowmik; Richard J. Hewitt; Wolfgang Lucht; Johan Rockström; Hans Joachim Schellnhuber; F. Allerberger; M. McCaffrey; S. S. Doe; A. Lenferna. 2020. "Social Tipping Dynamics for Stabilizing Earth's Climate by 2050." *Proceedings of the National Academy of Science* 117:2354–2365.

Park, Yong Chin, and Tom Pyszczynski. 2019. "Reducing Defensive Responses to Thoughts of Death: Meditation, Mindfulness, and Buddhism." *Journal of Personality and Social Psychology* 116:101–118.

Parks, Craig D., and Asako B. Stone. 2010. "The Desire to Expel Unselfish Members from the Group." *Journal of Personality and Social Psychology* 99:303–310.

Pascoe, Bruce. 2014. *Black Emu, Dark Seeds: Agriculture or Accident?* Broome, WA: Magabala Books Aboriginal Corporation.

Pavlovitz, John. 2020. "This Is How Holocausts Happen, How Nations Lose Their Humanity." *Blog Post*, January 9, https://johnpavlovitz.com/2019/08/30/this-is-how-holocausts-happen/?fbclid=IwAR12ODlpIuJY_IYw3cfVfk-Vrbao9Yn-kT8_ER1-otnk2dS7VwXDLQ_3zVw

Paxton, Robert O. 2004. *The Anatomy of Fascism.* New York: Knopf.

Peterson, Christopher; Steven Maier; Martin E. P. Seligman. 1993. *Learned Helplessness.* New York: Oxford University Press.

Peterson, Jillian, and James Densley. 2019a. "Who Are the Mass Shooters?" *Los Angeles Times*, August 6, A11.

———. 2019b. "Who Launches Religious Attacks?" *Los Angeles Times*, December 31, A9.

Phillips, Kevin. 2006. *American Theocracy: The Peril and Politics of Radical Religion, Oil, and Borrowed Money in the 21st Century.* New York: Penguin.

Piketty, Thomas. 2017. *Capital in the 21st Century.* Translated by Arthur Goldhammer. Cambridge, MA: Harvard University Press.

Pinker, Stephen. 2011. *The Better Angels of Our Nature: Why Violence Has Declined.* New York: Viking.

Policytensor. 2019. "Why Did Trump Win?" *Policytensor*, October 3, https://policytensor.com/2019/10/03/why-did-trump-win/#comment-38078

Popovich, Nadja; Livia Albeck-Ripka; Kendra Pierre-Louis. 2020. "The Trump Administration Is Reversing Nearly 100 Environmental Rules. Here's the Full List." *New York Times*, May 6, https://www.nytimes.com/interactive/2020/climate/trump-environment-rollbacks.html?action=clickandmodule=Newsandpgtype=Homepageandfbclid=IwAR2bKgLGwq8mXqqtXDPtFMwiYpq6cRdbUXIpn6iX4ywSeyT6EnD35k6kGzc

Putnam, Robert. 2000. *Bowling Alone: The Collapse and Revival of American Community.* New York: Simon and Schuster.

Ravitch, Diane. 2010. *The Death and Life of the Great American School System.* New York: Basic Books.

———. 2014. *Reign of Error: The Hoax of the Privatization Movement and the Danger to America's Public Schools.* New York: Vintage.

———. 2020. *Slaying Goliath: The Passionate Resistance to Privatization and the Fight to Save America's Public Schools.* New York: Knopf.

Rawls, John. 1971. *A Theory of Justice.* Cambridge: Harvard University Press.

———. 2001. *Justice As Fairness: A Restatement.* Cambridge, MA: Harvard University Press.

Reardon, Sara. 2018. "After the Violence." *Nature* 557:19–24.

Reicher, Stephen D.; Jay J. Van Bavel; S. Alexander Haslam. 2020. "Debate Around Leadership in the Stanford Prison Experiment: Reply to Zimbardo and Haney (2020) and Chan et al. (2020)." *American Psychologist* 75:406–407.

Reynolds, Arthur J.; Suh-Ruu Ou; Christina F. Mondi; Alison Giovanelli. 2019. "Reducing Poverty and Inequality Through Preschool-to-Third-Grade Prevention Services." *American Psychologist* 74:653–672.

Reynolds, Peter. 2020. *Life Without Darwin: Evolution, Religion and Postcapitalism.* Santa Barbara: Borderland North Publishing.

Rich, Frank. 2018. "The Original Donald Trump." *New York Magazine,* http://nymag .com/intelligencer/2018/04/frank-rich-roy-cohn-the-original-donald-trump.html? utm_source=fbandfbclid=IwAR33Wu1P-i5tIWSFrRGH1SrF5aaJqngPFpgBgJXb IkMkqLAUHO9RAIlxjzo

Robarchek, Clayton. 1989. "Primitive Warfare and the Ratomorphic Image of Mankind." *American Anthropologist* 91:903–920.

Robarchek, Clayton, and Carole Robarchek. 1998. *Waorani: The Contexts of Violence and War.* Fort Worth, TX: Harcourt Brace.

Rogers, Carl. 1961. *On Becoming a Person.* Boston: Houghton Mifflin.

Rolheiser, Ron. 2018. "Moral Outrage." Internet Posting by Author, April 15.

Rosenbaum, Ron. 2014. *Explaining Hitler: The Search for the Origins of His Evil.* New York: Da Capo Press, Perseus Group.

Ross, Michael L. 2012. *The Oil Curse: How Petroleum Wealth Shapes the Development of Nations.* Princeton: Princeton University Press.

Rovenpor, Daniel R.; Thomas C. O'Brien; Laura De Guissmé; Antoine Roblain; Peggy Chekroun. 2019. "Intergroup Conflict Self-Perpetuates via Meaning: Exposure to Intergroup Conflict Increases Meaning and Fuels a Desire for Further Conflict." *Journal of Personality and Social Psychology* 116:119–140.

Różycka-Tran, Joanna; Paweł Boski; Bogdan Wojciszke. 2015. "Belief in a Zero-Sum Game As a Social Axiom: A 37-Nation Study." *Journal of Cross-Cultural Psychology* 46:525–548.

Rummel, Rudolph. 1994. *Death by Government.* New Brunswick, NJ: Transaction Books.

———. 1998. *Statistics of Democide.* Munchen, Germany: LIT.

Sahlins, Marshall. 2008. *The Western Illusion of Human Nature.* Chicago: Prickly Paradigm Press.

Salaman, Redcliffe. 1985. *The History and Social Influence of the Potato.* 2nd edn. Edited by J. Hawkes. Cambridge: Cambridge University Press.

Salih, Kaziwa. 2019. "Kurdish Linguicide in the Saddamist State." *Genocide Studies International* 13:34–51.

Sapolsky, Robert. 2017. *Behave: The Biology of Humans at Our Best and Worst.* New York: Penguin.

———. 2018. "Double-Edged Swords in the Biology of Conflict." *Frontiers in Psychology* 9:2625 (online).

Saucier, Gerard, and Laura Akers. 2018. "Democidal Thinking: Patterns in the Mindset Behind Mass Killing." *Genocide Studies and Prevention* 12:80–97.

Savransky, Rebecca. 2017. "Poll: Most Republicans Say Colleges Have Negative Effect on the U.S." *The Hill*, July 10, http://thehill.com/homenews/news/341305-poll-most-republicans-say-colleges-have-negative-impact-on-us

SBS News. 2018. "Thousands of Batons, Cattle Prods and Handcuffs Ordered for China's 'Education' Camps." October 24, https://www.sbs.com.au/news/thousands-of-batons-cattle-prods-and-handcuffs-ordered-for-china-s-education-camps?fbcl id=IwAR1jxoM-Bv3w8ebQuTiaVJel-yjjvFsQm1u53aZP9-B8nQiiOiVLiTZ34S4

ScienceBeta. 2019. "Does Osteocalcin, Not Adrenaline, Drive Fight or Flight Response?" *ScienceBeta*, Sept. 12, https://sciencebeta.com/bone-fight-flight-res ponse/?fbclid=IwAR09yGV2zvCDPvPZDMYykmjSYC3PB-xZ1XUXkkxqhGrl pTHbIcIrMxyWewk

Scudder, Thayer. 2005. *The Future of Large Dams*. London: Earthscan.

Sen, Amartya. 1982. *Poverty and Famines: An Essay on Entitlement and Deprivation*. Oxford: Oxford University Press.

Shaw, Martin. 2013. *Genocide and International Relations: Changing Patterns in the Transitions of the Late Modern World*. Cambridge: Cambridge University Press.

Sherwin, Eoin; Seth R. Bordenstein; John L. Quinn; Timothy G. Doxon; John F. Cryan. 2019. "Microbiota and the Social Brain." *Science* 368:587.

Silverstein, Ken. 2018. "The Fear Factory: How Robert Mercer's Hedge Fund Profits from Trump's Hard-Line Anti-Immigrant Stance." *Yahoo! News*, November 2, https://www.yahoo.com/news/fear-factory-robert-mercers-hedge-fund-profits -trumps-hard-line-immigration-stance-090041709.html?fbclid=IwAR0jq3icmtv X7AuiKMJlGhGJXGW8pju1LBtP3VljEC5LHnd_8N59BvqEDB8

Smith, Adam. 1910 [1776]. *The Wealth of Nations*. New York: E. P. Dutton.

Snyder, Timothy. 2015. *Black Earth: The Holocaust As History and Warning*. New York: Tim Duggan Books.

———. 2018. *The Road to Unfreedom: Russia, Europe, America*. London: The Bodley Head (Division of Penguin Random House).

Soper, Spencer; Matt Day; Henry Goldman. 2020. "Amazon's Tale of Jealousy and Hubris." *Los Angeles Times*, February 10, A9.

Soto, Christopher J.; Oliver P. John. 2017. "The Next Big Five Inventory (BFI-2): Developing and Assessing a Hierarchical Model with 15 Facets to Enhance Bandwidth, Fidelity, and Predictive Power." *Journal of Personality and Social Psychology* 113:117–143.

Stanton, Gregory. 2013. "The Ten Stages of Genocide." *Posting, Genocide Watch Website*, http://genocidewatch.net/genocide-2/8-stages-of-genocide/

Staub, Ervin. 1989. *The Roots of Evil: The Origins of Genocide and Other Group Violence*. New York: Cambridge University Press.

———. 2003. *The Psychology of Good and Evil*. Cambridge: Cambridge University Press.

———. 2011. *Overcoming Evil: Genocide, Violent Conflict, and Terrorism*. New York: Oxford University Press.

Stavrou, David. 2019. "A Million People Are Jailed at China's Gulags. I Managed to Escape. Here's What Goes on Inside." *Haaretz*, October 17, https://www .haaretz.com/world-news/.premium.MAGAZINE-a-million-people-are-jailed-at-c hina-s-gulags-i-escaped-here-s-what-goes-on-inside-1.7994216?fbclid=IwAR1Z8 w4C5mPVHTcJxxxeJvDSIKMzaPF2CyMj1A8Ne4L-oP85zutFX3rxrsI

Stavrova, Olga, and Daniel Ehlebracht. 2016. "Cynical Beliefs About Human Nature and Income: Longitudinal and Cross-Cultural Analyses." *Journal of Personality and Social Psychology* 110:116–132.

Stedman, John Gabriel. 1988. *Narrative of a Five Years' Expedition Against the Revolted Negroes of Surinam*. Edited by Richard Price and Sally Price. Baltimore: Johns Hopkins University Press. (Orig. ms 1790; orig. publ. 1806–1813.)

Stenner, Karen. 2005. *The Authoritarian Dynamic*. Cambridge: Cambridge University Press.

Sterling, Joanna; John Jost; Richard Bonneau. 2020. "Political Psycholinguistics: A Comprehensive Analysis of the Language Habits of Liberal and Conservative Social Media Users." *Journal of Personality and Social Psychology* 118:805–834.

Sternberg, Robert J., and Karin Sternberg. 2008. *The Nature of Hate*. Cambridge: Cambridge University Press.

Stonich, Susan C. 1993. "I Am Destroying the Land!" In *The Political Ecology of Poverty and Environmental Destruction in Honduras*. Boulder: Westview.

Sun, Lena, and Janet Eilperin. 2017. "CDC Gets List of Forbidden Words: Fetus, Transgender, Diversity." *Washington Post*, December 15, https://www.washingt onpost.com/national/health-science/cdc-gets-list-of-forbidden-words-fetus-transg ender-diversity/2017/12/15/f503837a-e1cf-11e7-89e8-edec16379010_story.html? utm_term=.8aef9ac3d868

Tadmor, Carmit T.; Ying-yi Hong; Melody M. Chao; Ayala Cohen. 2018. "The Tolerance Benefits of Multicultural Experiences Depend on the Perception of Available Mental Resources." *Journal of Personality and Social Psychology* 115:396–426.

Tatz, Colin. 2018. "Seldom Asked, Seldom Answered: II(b) or not II(b)?" *Genocide Studies International* 11:216–227.

Tatz, Colin, and Winton Higgins. 2016. *The Magnitude of Genocide*. Santa Barbara: Praeger. (An imprint of ABC-CLIO.)

Taylor, Kathleen. 2009. *Cruelty: Human Evil and the Human Brain*. Oxford: Oxford University Press.

Te Brake, Wayne. 2017. *Religious War and Religious Peace in Early Modern Europe*. Cambridge: Cambridge University Press.

Tierney, John, and Roy E. Baumeister. 2019. *The Power of Bad, and How to Overcome It*. New York: Penguin (Allen Lane).

Timmerman, Jacobo. 2002. *Prisoner Without a Name, Cell Without a Number*. Madison, WI: University of Wisconsin Press.

Timmons, Heather. 2017. "The Three Ultra-Rich Families Battling for Control of the Republican Party." *Quartz*, online, December 5, https://qz.com/1085077/ mercers-vs-kochs-vs-adelsons-the-three-ultra-rich-families-battling-for-control-of -the-republican-party/

Tom, Joshua C. 2018. "Social Origins of Scientific Deviance: Examining Creationism and Global Warming Skepticism." *Sociological Perspectives* 612:341–360.

Tomasello, Michael. 2016. *A Natural History of Human Morality*. Cambridge, MA: Harvard University Press.

———. 2019. "The Origins of Morality." *Scientific American*, Sept., 70–75.

Tratner, Adam, and Melissa McDonald. 2020. "Genocide and the Male Warrior Psychology." In *Confronting Humanity at Its Worst: Social Psychological Perspective on Genocide*, Leonard S. Newman, ed. Oxford and New York: Oxford University Press. Pp. 3–28.

Traverso, Enzo. 2019. *The New Faces of Facism*. Translated by David Broder. French Original 2017. Verso.

Turchin, Peter. 2003. *Historical Dynamics: Why States Rise and Fall*. Princeton: Princeton University Press.

———. 2006. *War and Peace and War: The Life Cycles of Imperial Nations*. New York: Pi Press.

———. 2016. *Ages of Discord*. Chaplin, CT: Beresta Books.

Turchin, Peter, and Sergey Nefedov. 2009. *Secular Cycles*. Princeton: Princeton University Press.

Turner, James Morton, and Andrew C. Isenberg. 2018. *The Republican Reversal*. Cambridge, MA: Harvard University Press.

Turney-High, Harry Holbert. 1949. *Primitive War: Its Practices and Concepts*. Columbia, SC: University of South Carolina Press.

Van Lierop, Wal. 2019. "Yes, Fossil Fuel Subsidies are Real, and Protected by Lobbying." *Forbes*, December 6, https://www.forbes.com/sites/walvanlierop/201 9/12/06/yes-fossil-fuel-subsidies-are-real-destructive-and-protected-by-lobbying /?fbclid=IwAR1UvTyTvHXkQEvy8b-OSafhxbmoke4glmTtwvRWJeXHaUd-Z 4CXjAo8VoU#2e9f2c68417e

Vine, David. 2019. "No Bases? Assessing the Impact of Social Movements Challenging US Foreign Military Bases." *Current Anthropology* 60: Supplement 19:S158–S172.

Voorhees, Burton; Dwight Read; Liane Gabora. 2020. "Identity, Kinship, and the Evolution of Cooperation." *Current Anthropology* 61:194–218.

Waller, James. 2002. *Becoming Evil: How Ordinary People Commit Genocide and Mass Killing*. Oxford: Oxford University Press.

———. 2016. *Confronting Evil: Engaging Our Responsibility to Prevent Genocide*. New York: Oxford University Press.

Walters, Dale. 2017. *Fortress Plant: How to Survive When Everything Wants to Eat You*. Oxford: Oxford University Press.

Weisband, Edward. 2017. *The Macabresque: Human Violation and Hate in Genocide, Mass Atrocity and Enemy-Making*. Oxford: Oxford University Press.

———. 2019. "The Macabresque: Human Violation in Comparative Analytical Perspectives." *Journal of Genocide Research* 21:323–334.

Wenar, Leif. 2016. *Blood Oil: Tyrants, Violence and the Rules that Run the World*. Oxford: Oxford University Press.

Werner, Emmy; Ruth S. Smith. 1982. *Vulnerable but Invincible: A Longitudinal Study of Resilient Children and Youth*. New York: McGraw-Hill.

———. 2001. *Journeys from Childhood to Midlife: Risk, Resilience and Recovery*. Ithaca, NY: Cornell University Press.

Wiessner, Polly. 2019. "Collective Action for War and for Peace: A Case Study Among the Enga of Papua New Guinea." *Current Anthropology* 60:224–244.

Williams, Kipling D. 2007. "Ostracism." *Annual Review of Psychology* 58:425–452.

———. 2011. "The Pain of Exclusion." *Scientific American Mind*, January–February, 30–37.

Wilson, Sandra D. 1003 [2015]. *Hurt People Hurt People: Hope and Healing for Yourself and Your Relationships*. Grand Rapids, MI: Discovery House.

Wohlohl, Michael J. A.; Nassim Tabri; Eran Halperin. 2020. "Emotional Sources of Intergroup Atrocities." In *Confronting Humanity at Its Worst: Social Psychological Perspectives on Genocide*, Leonard S. Newman, ed. New York: Oxford University Press. Pp. 91–118.

Woodham-Smith, Cecil. 1962. *The Great Hunger*. New York: Harper and Row.

Worm, Boris. 2016. "Averting a Global Fisheries Disaster." *Proceedings of the National Academy of Sciences* 113:4895–4897.

Worm, Boris; Edward B. Barbier; Nicola Beaumont; J. Emmett Duffy; Carl Folke; Benjamin S. Halpern; Jeremy B. C. Jackson; Heike K. Lotze; Fiorenza Micheli; Stephen R. Palumbi; Enric Sala; Kimberley A. Selkoe; John J. Stachowicz; Reg Watson. 2006. "Impacts of Biodiversity Loss on Ocean Ecosystem Services." *Science* 314:787–790.

Wrangham, Richard. 2019. *The Goodness Paradox*. New York: Pantheon (Penguin Random House).

Xu, Chi; Timothy A. Kohler; Timothy M. Lenton; Jens-Christian Svenning; Marten Scheffer. 2020. "Future of the Human Climate Niche." *Proceedings of the National Academy of Sciences* 117:11350–11355.

Xunzi. 1999. *Xunzi*. Translated by John Knoblock. Changsha and Beijing, China: Hunan People's Publishing House and Foreign Language Press.

Zaki, Jamil. 2019. *The War for Kindness: Building Empathy in a Fractured World*. New York: Crown.

Zeki, Semir, and John Paul Romaya. 2008. "Neural Correlates of Hate." *PLoS One* 3:10:e3556.

Zimbardo, Philip. 2008. *The Lucifer Effect: Understanding How Good People Turn Evil*. New York: Random House.

———. 2018. "Philip Zimbardo's Response to Recent Criticisms of the Stanford Prison Experiment." *Blog*, June, http://www.prisonexp.org/response

Zimbardo, Philip, and Craig Haney. 2020. "Continuing to Acknowledge the Power of Dehumanizing Environments: Comment on Haslam et al. (2019) and Le Texier (2019)." *American Psychologist* 75:400–401.

Index

About the Authors

E. N. Anderson, PhD, is professor of anthropology, emeritus, at the University of California, Riverside. He received his PhD in anthropology from the University of California, Berkeley, in 1967. He has done research on ethnobiology, cultural ecology, political ecology, and medical anthropology, in several areas, especially Hong Kong, British Columbia, California, and the Yucatan Peninsula of Mexico. His books include *The Food of China* (1988), *Ecologies of the Heart* (1996), *Political Ecology of a Yucatec Maya Community* (2005), *The Pursuit of Ecotopia* (2010), *Caring for Place* (2014), *Everyone Eats* (2014), *Food and Environment in Early and Medieval China* (2014), and with Barbara A. Anderson, *Warning Signs of Genocide* (2013).

Barbara A. Anderson, DrPH, CNM, FAAN, is professor of nursing emerita, at Frontier Nursing University. She has done research on health care decision making among Cambodian refugees on the Cambodia border and among resettled refugees in the United States. She is a public health specialist and nurse-midwife with extensive academic teaching and program consultation. Her consultation work has focused on Southeast Asia and Africa. Her books include *Reproductive Health* (2005), *Caring for the Vulnerable* (2008, 2012, 2016, 2020), *Best Practices in Midwifery* (2012, 2017), *DNP Capstone Projects* (2015), *The Maternal Health Crisis in America* (*American Journal of Nursing* first place award in maternal health, 2019), and with E. N. Anderson, *Warning Signs of Genocide* (2013).

CPSIA information can be obtained
at www.ICGtesting.com
Printed in the USA
LVHW040325100123
736839LV00014B/337

9 781793 634610